M000044312

THE COMPLETE GUIDE

# GIN & TONIC

FOR THE PERFECT MIX

# GIN TONIC

FRÉDÉRIC DU BOIS & ISABEL BOONS

LANNOO

"The gin and tonic has saved more Englishmen's lives, and minds, than all the doctors in the Empire."

Winston Churchill

# PREFACE

## "I like large parties. They're so intimate. At small parties there's never any privacy."

Just like the character of Jordan Baker — played by Elizabeth Debicki in the 2013 film of *The Great Gatsby* — we love to throw a hell of a party. Don't misunderstand us, there is nothing wrong with an intimate party with friends, but in this book we are pulling out all the stops and won't let anyone go thirsty. It doesn't matter to us where and with whom you drink your gin & tonic, but what does fascinate us is how you take your gin & tonic. What comes out of your glass should dance on the tongue, extend the boundaries, and passion should triumph: So... Let's get this party started!

Where others finish, we will go further. Our book will answer your questions, and those that still burn on the lips of everyone who is passionate about gin & tonic: "Which gin do I combine with which tonic, and what garnish do I add?" Well, after reading this book you will be able to amaze your friends and foes with a heavenly gin & tonic. Perfectly mixed, using the right utensils, and the best tasting garnish 'popped' on top! Throughout the book you will discover more than twenty tonics and sixty gins. At the back you will find a comprehensive 'Gincyclopedia'.

This book is our homage to the immensely popular drink, and your guide on the quest for the ultimate gin & tonic. First, we will catapult you back in time and get thoroughly 'gin soaked' and then resume our journey and take you to 'tonic land'. Read and learn. Then we will take you into the passionate relationship between gin & tonic. We will blow you away with a cornucopia of information, guidelines and sensations. We will show you how to find your ideal match, and add the right garnish, too.

To make the party complete, we will be combining various meals with gin & tonic. We will discover that our favourite drink is at home in any situation, and can complement all kinds of recipes. We round up with twelve must-visit bars. After that, it is up to you: taste, discover and experience. We are more than happy to accompany you on your journey to find your ultimate gin & tonic!

This book is for those who never leave a party early, for those who watch a concert to the very end. For the truly individual, or those who aspire to be so. For those who like to slowly savour, or those who thrive on a snap decision. For those in search of inspiration and information, or those who just want to use the book to get pleasantly sozzled. For those who are in search of a new love, or those who have already found their love.

But first and foremost, for those who prize passion above all.

For all who literally 'live life to the fullest' ...

Cheers to us!

*Note:*
*The author F. Scott Fitzgerald was a notorious gin lover...*

# GIN: SOME HISTORY

## OR HOW THE JUNIPER BERRY CHANGED THE WORLD...

Before gin, there was genever or jenever. In Belgium it is called jenever with a 'j', while in the Netherlands it is often referred to as genever with a 'g'. The history of gin is not an entirely untroubled one: it is a story of courage, calamity and mishap, but also of new innovations, insights and trends, which continues right up to the present day. Whisky makes us think of the Scottish Highlands, rum conjures up pirates and the shipping trade and vodka whispers of Siberian winters, but the story of gin spreads from the Middle East to Europe and America, it is a history that completely changed the world...

### BELGIUM OR THE NETHERLANDS

*'der naturen bloeme'*

Our favourite, gin, is based on a famous drink which has its origins in the Low Countries (now Belgium and the Netherlands). The first mention of the juniper berry can be found in *Der Naturen Bloeme*, (The Flowers of Nature) written by Jacob van Maerlant in 1269. This encyclopaedia applauds the juniper berry for its many medicinal properties. Van Maerlant writes about juniper berries cooked in wine and how it is used as a medicine against cramps and stomach pains. A century later, jenever appears again in a booklet, this time as a medicine to cure the plague; the author, Jan van Aalter, is also the first to mention the euphoric effects of jenever. Both Jacob and Jan happened to be Flemish although jenever is well-known both in Great Britain and America, and even today is still called 'Dutch Courage' or 'Holland Gin', referring to its Low Countries heritage. During the siege of Antwerp in 1585, many flee to the Netherlands, taking their beloved jenever with them. The following century sees Belgium burdened by prohibition, meanwhile however in the Netherlands, the Golden Age is dawning, allowing the production methods of gin to develop.

## YES, WE CAN...

As people become more familiar with distillation methods, they discover that spirits can be made from anything that ferments. You can just imagine the world of possibilities that unfolded, and during the 14th and 15th centuries a lot of enthusiastic experimentation takes place. In Poland and Russia they discover the delights of a new use for the potato, and in Ireland and Scotland they are busy with barley. In the Low Countries brandy is a term used for a whole range of different spirits. Excise reports from 1492 show that significant amounts of grain-based spirits, particularly rye, are very commonly distilled. In 1582, the first technical description for distilling spirits from grain appears: *Guide to Distilling Korenbrandewijn* (corn brandy) by Casper Jansz.

## THE MYTH OF
## DOCTOR SYLVIUS

The 17th century — the Golden Age in the Netherlands: the Dutch East India Company has flourished to become the largest trading company in the world, Rembrandt is painting his masterpieces, and medical science is evolving fast. It is at this time that Doctor Sylvius (1614-1672), a professor at Leiden University, allegedly creates 'Dutch Gin'. However, we refute this claim. It is true that he used jenever as a medicine for kidney complaints and as a remedy for the plague, but it is highly unlikely that he was the inventor of gin. First and foremost, in the book by Philippus Hermanni, *Een Constelijck Distileerboec* from 1552, jenever or gin is mentioned as 'Aqua Juniperi', and this is 98 years before the good doctor was born. There are also references to jenever/gin found in a medieval English cookery book, and also in the play *The Duke of Milan*, first published in 1632 when Doctor Sylvius was still only nine years old.

### DUTCH COURAGE

It is during the thirty years' war (1618-1648), a far reaching conflict in which most European powers were embroiled, that English soldiers, brought in to deal with the Spanish forces and stationed in the southern Netherlands, are first introduced to jenever. These brave men certainly deserved a tipple before going into battle. Often however, the next day, the heroes found it hard to remember whom or what they had or had not beaten. And so they christen this 'Dutch Courage', ginniver, an Anglicization of jenever, which later becomes just gin. Upon returning home, they obviously take this habit back with them. Yet jenever is not completely unknown in Great Britain, and certainly familiar in London which, in 1571, provided a safe haven to 6,000 Flemish protestant refugees.

## WILLIAM OF ORANGE
## AND THE MERRY BREWERS

England, 1688: William of Orange III ascends the throne, marking the beginning of a new era. English society is undergoing a major turnaround, not least in their drinking habits. The new king almost immediately stimulates the production of English spirits, and it becomes possible for anyone to take up brewing gin without a licence. At the same time, import taxes on foreign drinks sky rocket. This results in an explosion in gin production as everyone takes up brewing.

### GIN CRAZE

'Blue Ruin', 'Ladies' Delight', 'Cuckolds' Comfort' or 'Madam Geneva', the new drug of the 18th century has many nicknames, and England is, as never before, in the grip of a drink craze. London in particular will never be as 'under the influence' as it was between 1720 and 1751, with this period often compared to the crack epi-

demic of the 1980s in America. And indeed, Londoners were almost permanently high on gin. At this time, gin is cheap and readily available, but of terrible quality. The malty complexity of the Dutch genever proves too much of a challenge for the local brewers, and often poor-quality grain is used to produce a neutral spirit, cut with oil of turpentine, oil of vitriol and alum. To mask the taste they use large amounts of sugar, limewater and rosewater. The consequences of this are devastating: gin is blamed for a number of woes, the rise in crime, prostitution and insanity, higher mortality rates and a fall in the birth rate, as a huge proportion of the city's population just drifts the streets from morning till night.

To give an idea of the extent of the impact of this opium of the people, here are a few facts:

- *In 1723, the death rate in London far outweighs the birth rate, and it will remain so for ten years.*
- *At one point, there are 7,044 recognized gin retailers and thousands of street sellers amongst a population of 600,000 Londoners.*
- *Between 1730 and 1749, 75% of children die before they reach the age of five.*
- *Between 1740 and 1742, there are two funerals for every christening.*
- *As many as 9,000 children die from alcohol poisoning in 1751.*
- *In 1733, almost 47 million litres of legal gin are produced in London, an equivalent of 53 litres of gin per person per year.*
- *In 1740, no less than half of all the beverage-serving establishments in London are so-called 'gin shops'.*

### WILLIAM HOGARTH'S GIN LANE (1697-1764)

This historic engraving perfectly illustrates just how bad things had become, and there is no better depiction of the havoc wreaked in London while in the grips of gin mania. It is easy to understand why reformers felt so desperate about the situation. *Gin Lane* is a busy street, full of scenes of misery: a carpenter pawns his tools for money to buy gin, a little further on an undertaker is placing the body of an emaciated woman in a coffin. An addict has hanged himself, while a mother feeds her child gin to lull it to sleep. And these depraved figures only form the back drop. In the foreground, amidst all the turmoil, a woman in a completely drunken stupor seems oblivious as her child slips out of her arms, about to fall over the balustrade.

## GIN ACTS

Almost as tragic as the stories of the effects of gin in the 18th century, were the comical, frantic and unsuccessful attempts of the government to get a grip on the consumption of gin. In the period between 1729 and 1751, the British Parliament introduces no less than eight different Gin Acts, some more successful than others, so let's just sum up the most important. In 1729, the first attempt is made to levy a tax on alcohol; however rich land owners appeal to their corruptible friends in high places, so that they are still able to sell their grain to the distilleries. Following a few further unsuccessful attempts, finally in 1736, Parliament passes a new Gin Act. It is also around this time that the name 'Old Tom Gin' first appears. The new Gin Act, motivated more by money than morals, places such a hefty tax on the serving of gin, that in reality the law is more like prohibition, and those who break the law face heavy fines or even a prison sentence. The result of this is to drive the whole industry underground. Despite strong enforcement by the authorities, Londoners do not yield and the Gin Act is often simply ignored. Finally seven years later, the law is officially repealed. The Gin Act of 1751 is, however, more successful, as according to the law distillers may only sell their gin to bar owners with a licence. The licence fee is reasonable, and as a result of this action the quality of the gin also improves, with only gradual price increases. The Gin Craze slowly ebbs away by the end of the 19th century, so it is not too surprising that many of the great English distilleries date from this period.

### GIN PALACES

While the British Empire reshapes the world, the Industrial Revolution is completely restructuring Great Britain itself. The emergence of factories brings many people to the towns and cities, and the rise of the working classes challenges the old way of thinking. This new technological age sees mass production of furniture for the first time, oil lamps are being replaced by gas lighting and new ways of making glass are being developed. In other words, all these new innovations have led to the rise of the gin palaces: a new place where the working classes feel right at home, and probably nicer than their own homes at that. It is in 1829 that the first of these little gems appears, such as Thompson and Fearon's. The glamour and atmosphere of the gin palaces gives gin's image a boost and drinking is seen as more of a social occasion. Luckily...

### THE VERY FIRST
### GIN & TONIC

Meanwhile in India, there is also something happening which we mustn't overlook. Once again we have the soldiers to thank for a new evolution in drinking, or rather we can say with confidence, a revolution. At the beginning of the 19th century, the British of the East India Company were taking quinine to prevent malaria — and yes it is one of the main ingredients in tonic, but more about that later. To make the daily dose of quinine more palatable, they added water, sugar and lime, and it was soon followed by the addition of gin. So there we have it, the very first gin & tonic...

## FROM OLD TOM TO LONDON DRY

Due to the rise in excise duty and quality controls, the government now hopes that gin will never again be the 'killer' it once was. The premise is simple: gin is more expensive to make, and so therefore the quality of the gin also has to be better so as to justify the higher price. 'Old Tom' is now being sold in large barrels to retailers, who then add sugar. During the Gin Craze, gin was sweetened to cover up the poor quality, but now it is sweetened purely to cater to people's taste. With the advent of new distillation equipment, such as the Coffey Still, also known as the Continuous or Patent Still, the distillates produced are of a higher quality, and so the dry, unsweetened style of gins that we now know as London Dry Gin, come into being. The upper classes prefer this gin above its sweet counterpart, and when people first start to become aware of the concept of 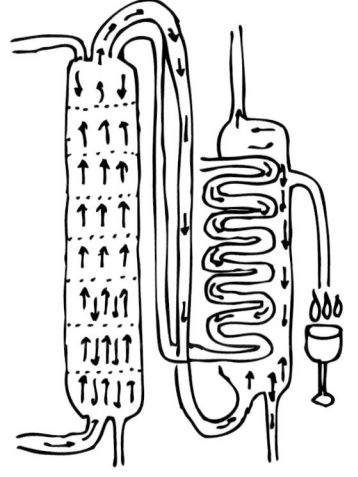 a healthy lifestyle during the Victorian era, the glory days of Old Tom are quickly over. The disappearance of Old Tom and the rise in popularity of dry gins is however, also thanks to the fact that the dry varieties lend themselves better to mixing. In 1860, the cocktail trend blows across from America and it isn't long before the fashion for mixing drinks is taken up throughout Europe. The English not only increase their exports of gin but also export their drinking habits, for example in World War I, and it is in this way that London Dry gin becomes known worldwide. In the 1920s and 1930s, gin also becomes popular in America, where it is regularly used as a base in cocktails, perhaps the most well-known of all being the Dry Martini.

## PROHIBITION AND 'BATHTUB GIN'

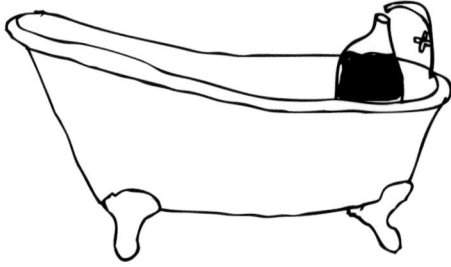

On 17th January 1920, American Congress passes the Volstead Act and prohibition comes into force. And what is forbidden becomes even more desirable. An entire generation of Americans plunge into criminality. Either they live in the speakeasies where they can drink illegal alcohol, or they make their own at home, and 'Bathtub Gin' becomes very popular. This despicable combination of industrial alcohol, glycerine and juniper oil is prepared in large bottles, too large to be filled under the tap in the sink, and so were filled from the tap in the bath. Sometimes the gin was also fermented and distilled in the bath itself, hence the name.

As a result of prohibition, English distilleries fear they would lose this important export market. But in fact the opposite proves to be true as exorbitant prices are offered for the real stuff. Prohibition comes to an end with President Franklin D. Roosevelt, and it is said that he even mixes the first legal martini in the White House himself.

## THE ROARING 20S:
## THE GLORY DAYS

Think glitter, glamour, new movements in music, fast cars, fashion, art and cocktails ... a lot of cocktails. *The Great Gatsby* by F. Scott Fitzgerald paints a perfect picture of what it was like in this era. Incidentally, did you know that F. Scott Fitzgerald had a weakness for Gin Rickey? A gin cocktail, where half a lime is first squeezed and then dropped into the glass, before topping up with soda water. It is rumoured that Fitzgerald was a gin lover because he believed that you couldn't detect gin on the breath. In the 20s, many bartenders leave America — as they are no longer allowed to ply their trade — and end up in London where they can share their skills. Cocktail parties in grand hotels are all the rage, replacing the more mundane afternoon tea. The driving force behind this party atmosphere: gin! The popularity of gin continues to grow and reaches its high point in the 50s and 60s with Hollywood stars such as Errol Flynn and Humphrey Bogart seldom seen without a Gin Martini in their hand.

### AND THEN CAME VODKA...

Gin continues to dominate the drinks world until after the 1960s, with probably half of all the existing cocktails using gin as their base at this time. And then vodka pokes its head around the corner, benefitting from good marketing and a hip image. Gin begins to be thought of as old-fashioned and stuffy. Luckily this old-fashioned connotation is no longer in question. Gin is back, and how!

## TODAY'S GIN CRAZE

It isn't until the end of the 20th century that the gin distilleries are able to head off the vodka tsunami. What took them so long? Maybe it was a lack of imagination, or maybe simply the time was not right. Big brands such as Tanqueray Ten and Bombay Sapphire set the tone, and create spin-offs of their brands which are more suited to the tastes of vodka drinkers: softer and rounder. Bombay Sapphire breathes new life into the market, raising its profile with a square blue bottle, which is appreciated by the trendy crowd and bartenders alike. At the same time, other distilleries are also beginning to stretch the boundaries, some brands using new ingredients, and some by re-interpreting the classic gin recipes. Halfway through the 'noughties', Hendrick's develops a Super Premium Gin, and many follow this example. Today, it is impossible to keep up, as almost every week a new brand comes to light.

Too much? Who knows, possibly...? But certainly, we are ecstatic about this resurrection.

## BUT WHERE DOES THIS NEW GIN CRAZE COME FROM?

Over the last five years or so, bartenders, chefs and enthusiasts in Spain have been inspired by gin, and in the last two years we have seen this trend also creeping into Belgium and Germany. In Holland this gin hype is mainly around Amsterdam, and for the Brits, gin is an historic product which they have loved for 400 years. Maybe it is due to British stoicism or pride, but it has to be said they don't seem too bothered about this sudden surge in interest, although of course the bartenders in the UK are cheering on this gin explosion, as it offers them more room to experiment and show off their talents. Another explanation may be the rise in our interest in food; switching our eating habits to top quality products, new tastes and flavours, all unquestionably stimulated by today's top chefs. Alongside the transformation on our plates, our perception of what goes into our glasses is also evolving in the wake of this gastronomic revolution. The mixing of all sorts of spirits and mixers, 'mixology', is currently reaching new

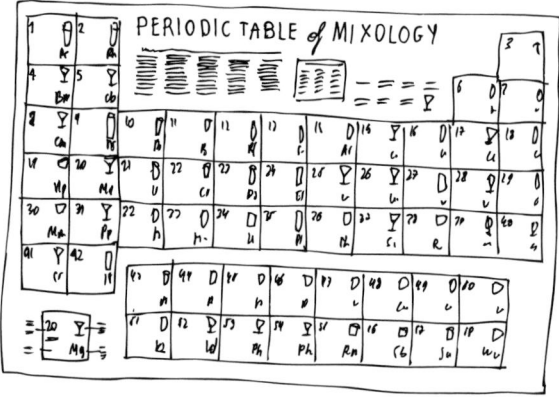

heights, and can certainly be referred to as gastronomy of the glass. Local bar culture is also playing its role, the new generation of bartenders are stimulating and motivating each other, by 'sharing' their knowledge. In the age of social media, it is the most natural thing in the world for them to let everyone know about new discoveries, experiments and knowhow. New bar concepts, or old but revitalised bar concepts are springing up all over the place. A good example of one of the concepts, growing daily in popularity, is the speakeasy. During the years of prohibition, going to a speakeasy guaranteed a fun — if illegal — 'night out on the town'. Nowadays (luckily), alcohol is no longer illegal and the term is used to describe a retro, 1920s ambiance bar, where mixed drinks of the highest quality are served. Speakeasies, like the originals, are shrouded in mystery: you may well have a bit of difficulty just finding the entrance, and even when you do, you may still not have actually reached the bar itself. Once inside however, you will be catapulted back in time, the décor, costumes and atmosphere will blow your mind. The drinks on offer are of the highest quality, and tell the story of the classic recipes.

Worth a try in our opinion — as long as you manage to find the way in... Hype? No, we believe that gin is here to stay, and this time for good. Sophisticated and well-thought-out, with tonic as its ally, gin will undoubtedly, once again, conquer the world.

# WHAT IS GIN?

## THE LEGAL CONDITIONS FOR GIN

European legislation — just as for Amaretto or Champagne — has rules with which gin must comply to be allowed to call itself gin. In the EU, gin has to have a minimum alcohol percentage of 37.5%. In the United States, the legal minimum alcohol percentage is set at 40%. The second condition is that the juniper berry has to have a prominent presence, notably 51% per production unit.

## THE DISTILLATION OF GIN: THE METHODS

### POT STILLED GIN

Of all the methods used, the pot still, also known as batch distillation, is the most traditional distillation technique. The neutral grain alcohol, which has to be heated to at least 96 °C, is put in the pot still and 'thinned down' with water before the botanicals are added. Depending on the individual recipe the alcohol will be warmed and left to stand and steep for hours, sometimes even days. At the appropriate moment, the distillation process begins by applying heat — and in the case of gin — by a steam jacket underneath the pot still. Following this, the distiller adds steam to bring

**POT STILL**

the alcohol to the boil, which will then reach the top of the pot, and immediately reduce the pressure. The vapours then pass through a swan neck tube to a water-cooled condenser. This first part of the distillate, also known as the 'heads', often contains impurities and is therefore drained into another vessel. The pure gin follows at various concentrations until eventually a strength of 80% is achieved. When this level reduces to 60% again, the impurities reappear. This last part of the distillate known as the 'tails' is likewise drained into separate vats. The next stage is to increase the steam pressure again, resulting in only water and the residue of the botanicals being left behind in the pot still. The distillation process is then repeated with the heads and the tails in another still which has a long neck and plates to remove the impurities, and so this part can also be used to make gin. After this, the final distillate is mixed with 90% alcohol and then finally brought back to the desired alcohol percentage.

### COLUMN DISTILLED GIN

Column distilled gin is a term associated with the invention of the Coffey still, and is also known as continuous distillation. Neutral grain alcohol (mostly wheat-based) is distilled to 96%. This distillate is then diluted with water to make the ideal alcohol percentage of 60%, to which herbs and spices are then added. Following this, it goes though the distillation process again, whereby the essential oils of the botanicals are released.

### Note:
*In both pot stilled gin and column distilled gin the master distiller can apply two methods to combine the alcohol with the other ingredients or botanicals. 'Racking' means that the botanicals are placed in a copper rack — a so called 'gin basket' — positioned above the still, where the hot alcohol vapours can extract the aromatic components of the botanicals. In 'steeping', the botanicals are placed in the spirit in the bottom of the still and allowed to stand and infuse.*

### VACUUM DISTILLED GIN

Vacuum distilled gin is produced differently to the previous methods. Instead of using heat for the distillation of the botanicals, cold distillation is used. With this method the pressure above the distillation solution is cooled to about -5 °C. At this freezing temperature the spirit vaporises. Following this, at -100 °C a type of probe is inserted into the still and the vapours return to liquid form. The flavours of the botanicals are now perfectly embedded in the spirit. The whole process takes around five to six hours. The great advantage to this method of cold distillation is that there are no 'heads' or 'tails', meaning virtually no wastage. But the real breakthrough is without a doubt in the taste of the gin. The theory is that in cold distillation the molecular structure of the botanicals is preserved and

so too, the true original taste is guaranteed.

Examples of gins developed in this way are Sacred Gin and Oxley Gin.

**Note:**

*Desmond Payne (master distiller at Beefeater) was the first to allow the botanicals to 'steep' in the alcohol for at least 24 hours prior to distillation, hence the name of their unconventional 'Beefeater24'. This technique has now been copied by countless gin makers. The time varies from distiller to distiller and can take anything from 6 to 24 hours.*

# GIN AND ITS BOTANICALS

The dominant juniper berry flavour is — as mentioned earlier — a legal requirement. As well as juniper berry, flavours such as orange or lemon peel, coriander seed, cardamom, caraway, cassia, cinnamon, angelica root and orris root, are commonly used botanicals in the new generation of gins. We have noticed that today, the average small batch (premium) gin uses some ten to twelve botanicals, almost becoming a standard, resulting in ever-increasing levels of quality.

Some of the most complex gins include Monkey 47 Gin with 47 botanicals, and Black Gin from the Gansloser Distillery with between 68 and 74 botanicals, depending on the source. These complex varieties are strongly reminiscent of herbal liqueurs such as Jägermeister. Both of these gins originate in the Black Forest region and will definitely appeal to a certain audience.

### JUNIPER BERRY

The signature of every gin. The use of the juniper berry determines the character and taste of each individual gin. The bittersweet flavours of pine, lavender and camphor are all identifiable in the juniper berry. The tree or bush grows almost everywhere in the northern hemisphere, and is even found growing at heights of up to 3,500 metres. The juniper used to create gin is always carefully selected and processed by the manufacturers. Each having their own personal preference, from Italy to Macedonia, hand-picked and handled with care. Once in the distillery, the juniper berries are matured for up to two years until the oil reaches the maximum aromatic potential.

### ANGELICA

Angelica is a biennial plant that, when growing in the wild, is most commonly found in moist, slightly acid, loamy soil. But it can also flourish just as well in the garden. According to legend, angelica can be used as a cure for the plague, or for protection against witchcraft. In gin, angelica root is used to make it 'dry'. The earthy notes help to support the botanic profile of a gin.

### CITRUS FRUITS

There is a definite trend to expand the citrus character of gin: bergamot orange, orange, lemon, lime, grapefruit, mandarin, etc. There is, however, a distinction made between the peel and the flesh or juice of the fruit.

### CARDAMOM

Cardamom is a member of the ginger family, with a sweet, sharp fragrance and tastes of bergamot, lemon and camphor. It originates from the Far East and is, after saffron and vanilla, the most expensive spice in the world. Before distillation, the seeds are crushed in order to fully release their warm, spicy aromas which are then infused into the gin.

### CARAWAY

Caraway is a biennial plant that is most commonly found in western Asia, Europe, and North Africa, where it grows in meadows, verges and dikes. Caraway seeds emit a spicy, sweet, aniseed flavour. Not to be confused with cumin, as the taste of caraway is much more pungent.

### CINNAMON

The cinnamon tree grows predominantly in Sri Lanka, but can also be found on Java, in Brazil and Egypt. The cinnamon tree will only grow in a tropical climate, and preferably on the coast. Cinnamon has a warm and spicy taste and has many culinary uses.

### CASSIA

Cassia is closely related to cinnamon and is similar in flavour and appearance. It is slightly hotter and sweeter than cinnamon and originates from Sri Lanka and China.

### CORIANDER SEED

Coriander seed is a spice which is a favourite in many kitchens, originating from the Middle East and the Mediterranean region. Coriander has always played a leading role in several gin recipes. During distillation, coriander seeds release a herby, sage and lemon taste.

### ORRIS ROOT

Orris root or iris root is used for many different purposes: in perfumes or potpourri, with the fragrance similar to violet. It is often included as one of the many ingredients in the Moroccan spice mix 'Ras el hanout'. In gin, orris root serves as a bonding agent for the other aromatics.

### LIQUORICE

The root of the liquorice plant is used throughout the world as a treatment for bronchitis. Gin distillers mainly source their liquorice from the Middle East. Liquorice contains sugars, bitters and a substance that produces its distinctive woody taste. The use of liquorice in gin softens the mouth feel.

### ALMONDS

The almond tree grows mostly in southern Europe. The bitter almond is used in gin, not the sweet variety. Almonds give gin a somewhat marzipan softness.

# TONIC: SOME HISTORY

## FROM MEDICINE TO PERFECT MIXER...

### 1638:
### THE MIRACULOUS CURE

Just like gin, tonic started life as a medicine. The legend takes us back to 17th century Peru. The countess Ana de Osorio del Chinchón is suffering from one of the most serious forms of the life-threatening disease, malaria. Her husband—whose unpronounceable name we will save you from—pleads with the local medicine man, desperate to find a cure for his wife's fever. Luckily the medicine man is feeling generous and gives

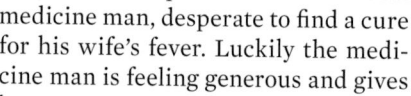

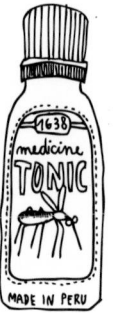

her a mysterious concoction to drink made from the bark of the native 'Quinquina' tree. The Countess recovers in miraculous fashion. In honour of the Countess and in celebration of her recovery, the Spaniards re-christen the Peruvian tree, and it is known from then on as the 'Cinchona' tree. They also eradicate the Incas, steal their gold and colonise their land!

### EXPORT TRADE BOOMS

Meanwhile, the Countess Ana, oozing with health, returns to her estate in Spain, taking a large quantity of the healing tree bark with her. The fame of this magical substance—which we now know as quinine—quickly spreads throughout Europe, and this wonderful medicine also cures Charles II of England and the son of Louis XIV of France. Quickly the powder form of the tree bark becomes worth more than gold, and demand soon outweighs supply. Suddenly, the so-called 'fever tree' is threatened with extinction.

## 1850:
## SMUGGLING WAR

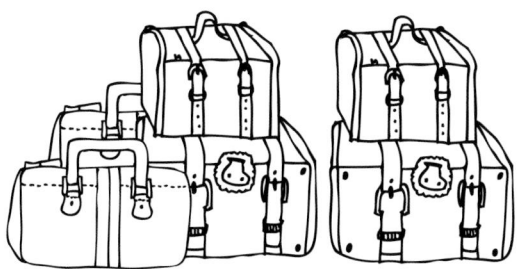

In the middle of the 19th century, the British and the Dutch come up with a splendid idea: to smuggle the seeds of the 'fever tree' out of Latin America. The British try planting the trees in their own colonies in India and Ceylon, but are unsuccessful in producing quality quinine. The Dutch, however, fare better in their colony Java, where the trees grow and flourish to produce good quality quinine. By 1918, Java has become the biggest producer of quinine in the world.

### SWEET MEDICINE

Meanwhile, quinine starts to be used to also prevent, as well as cure malaria. At this time of colonisation, malaria runs rife, and so quinine is popular stuff. The

bitter taste almost 'throws a spanner in the works' but it is the British occupiers in India who start to mask the bitter taste of the quinine with sugar and dilute it with water. Soldiers and their commanders are given this medicine daily, and it is not too long before some spirited soul is inspired to add gin to the mix. This rekindles the flame of enthusiasm, which has burned brightly ever since.

### 1858:
### FIRST COMMERCIAL TONIC

It is the shrewd British businessman, Erasmus Bond who first sees an opportunity in this trend among the British soldiers and officers, and in 1858 he produces the first commercial tonic: "improved aerated tonic liquid". His invention is first seen as a health product, but it doesn't take long before this first tonic moves from the medicine chest to the drinks cabinet.

### 1944:
### SCIENCE KICKS IN

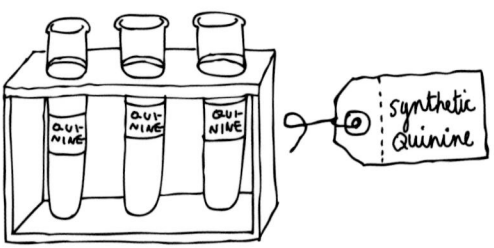

Up until World War II, Indonesia produced more than 95% of the world's quinine. This however, comes to an abrupt end when the Japanese occupy Java. This results once again in a shortage of quinine for medical use, and so scientists are brought in to develop a synthetic alternative. By 1944, this synthetic variant has become reality. Synthetic quinine is still in use up to this very day in the creation of certain types of tonic, but it goes without saying that the synthetic version, at the very least, tastes different to the natural form.

## TONIC TODAY

Gin is back; maybe bigger than ever. The evolution of more sophisticated and aromatic gin varieties logically demands that mixers are also elevated to a new level. A new generation of tonics — undoubtedly with a view to forming the perfect partnership with gin — have been making their entrance over the last few years. And we can safely say they have been glittering debuts, raising the bar even higher for the iconic long drink.

Gin & tonic is the perfect example of a successful marriage. A marriage that will last forever. And let's face it; separating this couple is just unthinkable...

# WHAT IS TONIC?

Tonic is a carbonated soft drink, whose bitter taste comes from the addition of our now well-known — well, if you have read the last few pages at least — quinine. As well as the quinine, tonic water is flavoured with sugar or sweeteners, and is often further enhanced by the addition of various fruit extracts. But let's get back to the quinine. Are you planning a trip to the tropics? Imagine: a few tonics, or better still, a few gin & tonics and you are protected against malaria. It is possible, but only if you consume two litres of tonic, containing natural quinine, per day, equal to ten gin & tonics. Whether that is a good idea or not, we will have to leave up to you.

# GIN & TONIC
# THE IDEAL MATCH

Finding the ideal match rests on one basic principle, and that is the right combination of tastes. That is why we are categorizing the tonics as well as the gins according to their flavours. To create an explosive combination in your glass, we will blend the tastes by mixing the various types of gin with the most appropriate tonic.

And indeed, we are beginning with the tonic. Not that we want to be 'contrary' or attempt to paddle upstream, and we are certainly not suggesting a switch to 'tonic & gin'; not at all, the one and only reason is to make it easier for you. Consider it a warm up, or maybe a safeguard against too many premature hangovers, but above all, there can be no gin & tonic without the tonic. Although it is fair to say that tonic is, and will always be, the secondary ingredient in our favourite cocktail, but just as with gin, there are many differences in the quality and tastes. Failing to give some thought to the tonic is like not bothering about putting the right sort of fuel in the engine of your car.

With the re-birth, and explosion in the popularity of gin, tonic is similarly enjoying a serious resurgence. Tonic will always be a dominant flavour in our gin & tonic, and that is why we begin with this ode to tonic, for once bringing it out of gin's shadow. You will be introduced to an entire new generation of tonics, and believe us when we say, it will be both a fascinating and pleasurable experience, forming the basis of all your future creations. And maybe yes, we actually do enjoy paddling upstream, just a little...

# TONIC: CATEGORIZATION

NEUTRAL    AROMATIC

FRUITY / FLORAL

For the perfect gin & tonic it is first important to know which flavours are in your tonic, and when armed with this knowledge you will be able to amaze your friends and foes alike. OK, gin is our protagonist, but a decent knowledge of tonic is also essential for creating your ultimate gin & tonic later. We categorize the new generation of tonics on the basis of their taste: **neutral**, **aromatic** and **fruity/floral**.

As we want to give you as detailed an overview as possible, we will not be concentrating too much on the big brands such as Kinley Tonic, Nordic Mist Tonic Water and Schweppes Indian Tonic. Instead we will focus in depth on the new generation of tonics, which mostly make use of natural ingredients and, as a consequence, really allow the gin to shine through.

So fasten your seatbelts and prepare for takeoff... Here we go!

# NEUTRAL
# TONICS

# ABBONDIO
# TONICA
# VINTAGE EDITION

### ORIGIN

In business for over 120 years, Abbondio is one of the oldest drinks producers in Italy. Above all, this brand is seen as the most prestigious in the country. Angelo Abbondio set up his soft drinks factory in Tortona in 1889 and paid special attention to quality and traditional recipes. The pin-up pictures used on the bottles are quite striking. The Abbondio tonic was created at the beginning of the 20th century and was originally called 'bitter gazzosa'.

### INGREDIENTS

carbonated water ....................................................
cane sugar ..............................................................
quinine ...................................................................
natural flavourings ...............................................

### TASTE AND FLAVOUR

The traditional formula seamlessly integrates the sour taste of the lemons with the cane sugar. Lightly carbonated and completely free of genetically modified products.

# BRITVIC
# INDIAN
# TONIC WATER

### ORIGIN

In the middle of the 19th century, a British chemist began to experiment with the making of soft drinks at home. A little while later, James MacPherson & Co bought the recipes and introduced the drinks into the United Kingdom, under the name of British Vitamin Products. In 1971, the name changed from British Vitamin Products to Britvic and so the Britvic brand was born.

### INGREDIENTS

carbonated water....................................................
sugar ......................................................................
citric acid................................................................
flavourings: including quinine.............................
preservatives: potassium sorbate.......................
saccharin.................................................................

### TASTE AND FLAVOUR

On the nose, a real tonic: very lively citrus scent. In the mouth, sparkling with a dry and bitter finish. Big bubbles.

# FEVER-TREE
# INDIAN TONIC
# WATER

### ORIGIN

The story begins with Charles Rolls, the man who brought Plymouth Gin back onto the market. After following a tonic-tasting course in 2000 with Tim Warrillow, they concluded that a lot of mixers used sodium benzoate or similar chemical substances as preservatives. Additionally, the use of cheap orange flavourings and artificial sweeteners jumped out at them, leading the men to exclaim "We can safely call this combination an attack on the taste buds". It was following this experience that the seeds of a simple yet brilliant idea began to grow: a gin & tonic is, after all, ¾'s tonic, why then is so little thought given to that tonic?! Fever-Tree Indian Tonic Water was launched in Great Britain in 2005 with the name deriving from the colloquial name for the Cinchona tree, the source of quinine. To do their tonic justice, Charles and Tim went in search of the best possible quality quinine, which they found in eastern Congo. Fever-Tree is therefore a tonic of premium quality, not only being served in seven out of the top ten restaurants in the world, but also in more than thirty countries worldwide.

Sounds like a 'good' idea...

## INGREDIENTS

spring water ..............................................................
cane sugar..............................................................
citric acid ..............................................................
natural flavours ......................................................
natural quinine ......................................................

Fever-Tree Indian Tonic Water is made using a mix of eight botanical flavours, including rare ingredients such as extract of marigold and sour orange from Tanzania. Lemons from Sicily, thyme and rosemary from Provence in France, ginger from Nigeria and Ivory Coast... Need we say more?
Fever-Tree is made by 100% natural production methods and uses no artificial sweeteners or preservatives.

## TASTE AND FLAVOUR

The taste can be called, at the very least, soft. The authentic ingredients and production techniques from the world of perfumers provide a pure and subtle tonic with a sparkle similar to that in champagne. Refreshing, with a clear tint of citrus, perfectly supported by the natural bitterness of the quinine. The clean finish and the absence of a sticky mouth make this tonic a top notch mixer.

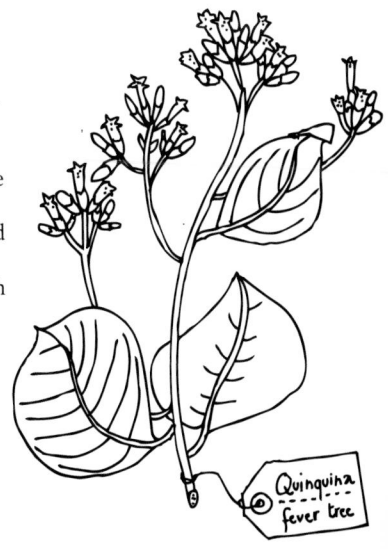

Quinquina
fever tree

# J.GASCO
# INDIAN TONIC

## ORIGIN

This tonic has its origin in a bizarre dream J.Gasco had during his expedition to the forests of French Guiana, in search of the legendary green anaconda. The environmentalist from Piemonte in Italy was awoken one night by a dream, in which an obscure figure offered him a fantastically delicious drink. He couldn't get the dream out of his head and dedicated the rest of his life to recreating this magical drink. Today, J.Gasco's traditional recipes are still used as the basis for J.Gasco mixers.

## INGREDIENTS

carbonated water......................................................
sugar ........................................................................
quinine ....................................................................
citrus essence..........................................................

## TASTE AND FLAVOUR

A typically neutral tonic, perfect for use as a mixer

# ORIGINAL
# PREMIUM TONIC

**ORIGIN**

Original Tonic Water Classic is produced by
Magnifique Brands in Madrid.

**INGREDIENTS**

carbonated water ....................................................
sugar .....................................................................
quinine ..................................................................
citrus.....................................................................
natural flavourings ...............................................

**TASTE AND FLAVOUR**

Crystal clear in appearance with a natural
aroma and a big bubble. Lightly sweet in the
beginning with hints of lemon and orange.

# SEAGRAM'S PREMIUM TONIC

## ORIGIN

The Seagram's brand came to life in the distillery of Joseph E. Seagram & Sons in Waterloo, Ontario, and takes its inspiration from the rugged Canadian wilderness. In 1928, Joseph E. Seagram & Sons was acquired by the Distillers Corporation Limited of Samuel Bronfman. After the death of Joseph Seagram, the distillery simply became known as Seagram Company Ltd., and so it is often wrongly claimed that Samuel Bronfman was the founder of Seagram. Over the years, Seagram Company Ltd. also acquired many shares in media companies such as Universal Studios, so it is somewhat surprising that Frankenstein wasn't saddled with alcohol problems... In 2000, the French concern Vivendi, gained a majority share in Seagram which heralded the end of the Canadian company. After the merger of Vivendi Universal, the various beverage divisions were sold in both public and closed auctions to PepsiCo, Diageo and Pernod Ricard. Acquired by Seagram in 1999, PolyGram merged with another Seagram music concern, MCA Music Entertainment to become Universal Music Group. Universal

## INGREDIENTS

sparkling water ........................
fructose syrup..........................
citric acid.................................
quinine .....................................
potassium sorbate...................
sodium......................................

## TASTE AND FLAVOUR

Complex and aromatic.
Spicy tints are clearly present.

Studios was then incorporated into Vivendi Universal Entertainment, later taken over by General Electric, and merged to become NBC Universal. Now enough of the film industry and back to the lesson. In 2002, the Coca-Cola Company acquired the mixer range, including Seagram's Premium Tonic Water, from Diageo and Pernod Ricard. And yet we are still not there... as far as gin is concerned. In 2006, Pernod Ricard announced plans to close Seagram's distillery in Lawrenceburg, Indiana. The distillery was temporarily taken over by CL Financial who, in turn, also went bankrupt, and from then on, the government took control of the company. Finally in 2011, MGP from Atchison, Kanas bought the distillery.

In an interview with *Globe and Mail*, Charles Bronfman, the son of Samuel Bronfman, declared: "The decisions that were made, led to Seagram becoming what it is now; they were a disaster, are a disaster, and will be a disaster..."

# SCHWEPPES
# PREMIUM TONIC

### ORIGIN

In their premium range, Schweppes choose
a formula based on 100% natural sugars and
ingredients from 100% natural sources. With
this premium tonic, Schweppes tickle all the
taste buds.

### INGREDIENTS

carbonated water ...................................................
sugar .......................................................................
citric acid ..............................................................
natural flavours ....................................................
quinine ...................................................................

### TASTE AND FLAVOUR

The formula guarantees the bubbles you
would expect in Schweppes. This neutral
tonic with a hint of lime gives a subtle and
direct taste.

ORIGINAL
PREMIUM MIXER

# THOMAS HENRY TONIC WATER

## ORIGIN

In 1773, the name Thomas Henry, a well-known apothecary, could already be found on the label of a bottle in Manchester. And, like most apothecaries, he loved to experiment. Fortunately for us, as it was thanks to his experiments that the very first carbonated soft drink was born. Perhaps without Thomas Henry we would never have had our favourite, gin & tonic. Today, Thomas Henry is a German company, which makes many a Berlin bartender's heart beat faster. They really know how to throw a party in Berlin, and they are only too pleased to share it with the rest of the world. Sebastian Brack and Norman Stievert are now the inspiration behind Thomas Henry, after all these years. They may not be apothecaries, but they are soft drinks fanatics, and it has to be said, real marketing boys. They have managed to keep their recipe secret and launched their Tonic Water, amongst others, at the end of 2010.

## INGREDIENTS

natural mineral water ...........................................
sugar .....................................................................
carbonated water ..................................................
citric acid ..............................................................
cinchona bark extract quinine .............................

## TASTE AND FLAVOUR

It is safe to say that Thomas Henry Tonic Water is full of flavour. The unusually high quinine content gives an archetypal bitter taste. However the taste does not linger too long and it is refreshing, pure and surprisingly soft. A grown up tonic with extra freshness. The extract of cinchona bark quinine ensures the individual character of Thomas Henry Tonic Water.

# 6 O'CLOCK
# INDIAN TONIC WATER

6 | 00

## ORIGIN

The story of 6 O'Clock begins with gin, namely the recipe of Edward Kain, innovator, inventor and, above all, adventurer. Edward was a ship engineer in the 19th century, indeed the century in which malaria claimed many victims. Edward and his colleagues drank tonic water during their voyages to protect against malaria, and one fine day, Edward came up with the fantastic idea to add gin to the tonic. Hallelujah! Legend has it that from that day forward, every day at 6pm Edward would partake in a gin & tonic, thus the name 6 O'Clock. It was Edward's great grandson, Michael Kain, who years later brought 6 O'Clock gin and its partner tonic onto the market and developed the idea of creating the perfect match. 6 O'Clock is made in the Bramley and Cage distillery, a small producer in Great Britain. Their strategy is clear: You can't buy the gin without the tonic, or the other way around. Moreover, the gin and the tonic are only offered to bars and restaurants within Great Britain. Bramley and Cage are also developing a sloe gin.

## INGREDIENTS

sparkling water .............................................................
extract of lemon and lime ......................................
citric acid ......................................................................
sugar ..............................................................................
natural quinine ..........................................................

6 O'Clock tonic contains no artificial sweeteners, or other flavourings.

## TASTE AND FLAVOUR

The pure taste is due to the use of natural quinine, with an exceptional twist of citrus. Beautifully balanced with a clear nose of lemon. A full-bodied tonic but surprisingly fresh.

# AQUA MONACO
# TONIC WATER

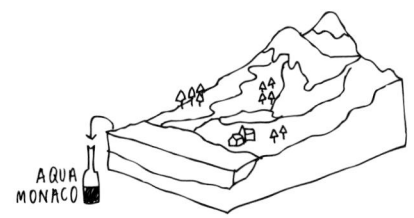

## ORIGIN

The basis of this tonic is Aqua Monaco, a sodium-free water extracted from the 'Münchner Schotterebene'. The what? Well, the Münchner Schotterebene is a gravel bed that was formed millions of years ago, caused by the effects of glaciers in the Alps. The ice flowed off the glaciers, scraping over the ground and taking a mass of rock pieces and other debris along with it. When the glacier melted, the water was trapped in the rocky layers of the gravel bed. Today, the water used for Aqua Monaco Tonic Water is obtained from the 'Silenca Quelle' (a source formed by glacial water) of the privately owned brewery Schweiger who use it to brew their beer. The story behind the name Aqua Monaco is simple, but worth telling. The Italian for the capital of Bavaria is 'Monaco di Baviera' and the sound of the name suits the people particularly well. It is fresh and appealing, and reflects the spirit of the city perfectly: uncomplicated and brimming with confidence.

## INGREDIENTS

natural spring water................................................
a little sugar.........................................................
quinine citric acid.................................................
carbon dioxide.....................................................
sage .....................................................................
Chinotto orange .................................................

## TASTE AND FLAVOUR

By using the purest of pure water, the best raw materials and a substantial reduction of the sugar content, the result is a particularly fine and delicious tonic. Very refreshing and brought to life by a slight acidity and a pleasant note of quinine. Extra carbon dioxide is added for that little extra sparkle.

# AROMATIC
# TONICS

# FEVER-TREE MEDITERRANEAN TONIC WATER

### ORIGIN

Fever-Tree Mediterranean followed — along with seven other Fever-Tree mixers — a few years after the launch of the original version. For the complete Fever-Tree story, see the neutral tonics section.

### INGREDIENTS

spring water ...............................................................
cane sugar ...............................................................
citric acid ...............................................................
natural flavourings ...............................................................
natural quinine ...............................................................
lemon oil from Sicily ...............................................................
geranium ...............................................................
rosemary ...............................................................
mandarin ...............................................................

### TASTE AND FLAVOUR

On the nose, clear aromas of thyme, with citrus and a hint of rosemary. The soft bitterness of the natural quinine and the elegant tastes of the herbs and citrus are accompanied by beautiful champagne-like bubbles.

# FENTIMANS TONIC WATER

## ORIGIN

In 1905, the Englishman Thomas Fentiman, using a traditional recipe which had been thrust under his nose as security on a loan, began brewing a botanical ginger beer. He started by grinding up ginger roots and boiled them in copper kettles to release the flavours. This syrup was then fermented in wooden barrels with brewer's yeast, sugar and botanicals such as ginger, juniper berry, veronica and yarrow extract. The loan was never repaid and so Thomas became the owner of this unique recipe and, with the aid of a horse and cart, he brought his ginger beer to the people. He bottled the beer in stone jars stamped with a picture of his dog 'Fearless'. Why his dog, I hear you ask? Well, Thomas was extremely proud of his dog, having twice won the prize for the most obedient dog at the famous dog show 'Crufts'. The depiction of Thomas' trusted four-footed friend is still used today in Fentimans logo. Now, more than 100 years later, the brewing process has of course been modernised. However, the recipe itself remains virtually unchanged, including fermenting the mixture for a week in a vat. Due to the addition of the natural flavourings and herbs, the alcohol percentage of Fentimans Tonic Water is reduced to less than 0.5% and therefore can be legally sold as a soft drink. So, never call Fentimans 'just a mixer'.

## INGREDIENTS

soda water ................................
sugar ..........................................
citric acid ..................................
natural flavourings ..................
quinine ......................................
spice infusions such as juniper berry, cinnamon and kaffir lime leaf

Fetimans Tonic Water is, without exception, manufactured using 100% natural ingredients such as Sicilian oranges

## TASTE AND FLAVOUR

The tonic has the spicy nose of lemon, lemongrass and ginger. As Fentimans Tonic Water is created with less quinine than some of its colleagues there is no 'metallic' aftertaste. The tonic clearly has many layers which are subtly released and brought to the forefront.

# ORIGINAL
# PREMIUM TONIC BLUE

---

### ORIGIN

Original Tonic Water Blue is produced
by Magnifique Brands in Madrid.

### INGREDIENTS

carbonated water ...............................................
sugar ....................................................................
quinine ................................................................
citrus....................................................................
grapefruit............................................................

### TASTE AND FLAVOUR

Clear blue in appearance with a natural
fragrance and a small bubble. Fresh tones
of lime and sour lemon in the beginning,
subsequently complemented by the bitter
quinine taste, which is then followed by
subtle hints of orange and grapefruit.

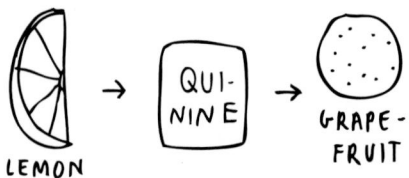

# FRUITY/ FLORAL TONICS

# SCHWEPPES PREMIUM TONIC PINK PEPPER

PINK PEPPER

### ORIGIN

For their premium range, Schweppes choose a formula based on 100% natural sugars and ingredients from 100% natural sources.

### INGREDIENTS

carbonated water...................................................
sugar ........................................................................
citric acid................................................................
natural flavourings ...............................................
quinine ....................................................................
pink pepper............................................................

### TASTE AND FLAVOUR

An adventurous taste with a high pepper content enhancing the flavours of the juniper berry in the gin. Pink pepper has been carefully studied, as it highlights the essence of an alcoholic drink and adds a fruity and rebellious touch.

# GENTS
# SWISS ROOTS
# PREMIUM TONIC

### ORIGIN

This tonic is produced by the start-up company Gents GmbH in Zurich. Its creator is journalist and communications expert Hans Georg Hildebrandt, alongside senior specialist Patrick Zbinden, the young chef Ralph Schelling and Markus Blattner, barman at the Widder Hotel, who lend their support to the basis of this tonic. The name 'Gents' was inspired by a local herb variety, the yellow gentian. This herb is widely used in a number of drinks from the Alpine region.

### INGREDIENTS

carbonated water......................................................
sugar beet from Switzerland..............................
lemon essence from Sicilian lemons.................
quinine from Peru.....................................................
extract from the yellow gentian.........................

### TASTE AND FLAVOUR

The harmonious mix of the ingredients ensures a good balance of flavours. Full and pleasantly sleek in the mouth, with a light floral hint.

# THOMAS HENRY ELDERFLOWER TONIC

ELDERFLOWER

---

## ORIGIN

Thomas Henry Elderflower Tonic is the most recent to be launched by the company. For more on the history of Thomas Henry, see the entry under 'Neutral Tonics'. The medicinal properties of elderflower have been known for centuries, but nowadays it is also used for many other purposes, including as an ingredient in liqueurs or cocktails and even in champagne. Thomas Henry Elderflower Tonic is also the ideal gin partner, as the floral touch wonderfully balances the juniper flavours.

## INGREDIENTS

natural mineral water.............................................
sugar .......................................................................
carbonated water..................................................
citric acid...............................................................
flavourings: quinine .............................................
elderflower.............................................................

## TASTE AND FLAVOUR

Light and floral

# INDI BOTANICAL TONIC

## ORIGIN

Indi Tonic was launched in 2012 by Indi & Co and has its origins in Seville, Spain. In the quest for the perfect mixer, the Spanish developers have delved into their own culinary traditions, flavours and colours. In the Guadalquivir valley they have been drying aromatic herbs, oranges and lemons for hundreds of years, both for medicinal as well as culinary use. As it was not their intention to develop a medicine for headaches, the idea for Indi Tonic began to grow in the passionate minds of the Andalusians. By mixing age-old traditions with exotic ingredients like quinine and vanilla, the tonic is almost ready for the glass... almost...

The production in the Spanish village of El Puerto Santa Maria begins with a process of softening the botanical ingredients by macerating or soaking in cold water and alcohol. The resulting liquid is then distilled in a copper distillation kettle at a low temperature. This allows for a slower and finer distillate which ensures that the tastes and flavours are faithfully captured. Finally, purified water, white sugar and cane sugar are added.

## INGREDIENTS

purified water .........................................................
quinine .................................................................
sugars..................................................................
botanical spices: orange peel from Seville, kalonji (black cumin from India), kewra (plant), cardamom from India

Indi Tonic is completely crafted by hand, and only contains 100% natural ingredients.

## TASTE AND FLAVOUR

Intense citrus with a hint of orange peel, setting the tone for perfect harmony with aromatic notes of cardamom and freshness from the kewra flower. Black cumin subtly prickles the tongue and perfectly combines with both the bitterness of the quinine and the sweetness of the sugars. Indi Tonic can certainly be consumed on its own, although we prefer the combination with gin.

# ORIGINAL
# PREMIUM TONIC PINK

### ORIGIN

Original Tonic Water Pink is produced by
Magnifique Brands in Madrid.

### INGREDIENTS

carbonated water ...................................................
sugar ........................................................................
quinine .....................................................................
citrus........................................................................
red fruits .................................................................

RED FRUIT

### TASTE AND FLAVOUR

This fruity tonic is soft pink in colour and
naturally fragrant. A slightly larger bubble
than the original version and with a perfect
balance between bitter and sweet. The red
fruits slowly emerge and then explode in the
finish, with perfectly integrated citrus tones.

# Q TONIC

### ORIGIN

Q Tonic is the jewel in the crown of Q Drinks. The tonic was developed in Brooklyn, NY, by founder Jordan Silbert. The product is bottled in Worcester, Massachusetts. In 2002, Silbert began the process of developing, as it were, his tonic in his own garage, driven by his belief that too many soft drinks use synthetic quinine. He ordered the bark of the Cinchona tree online from Peru, for a mere ten dollars, which turned out to be a very good investment. In 2004, he asked for specialist help to further develop the recipe, leading to the addition of agave nectar to make the recipe sweeter. Q drinks finally opened for business in 2006.

### INGREDIENTS

spring water with a high mineral content.........
citric acid ................................................................
Peruvian cinchona bark.......................................
Mexican agave syrup...........................................

### TASTE AND FLAVOUR

Q Tonic is soft yet pungent on the nose and is lightly salty in character. The tonic is certainly not sweet allowing the taste of the gin to remain unmasked. The earthy tone ensures that the quinine does not dominate the foreground.

UNITED KINGDOM

# SCHWEPPES
# PREMIUM TONIC
# ORANGE BLOSSOM
# & LAVENDER

## ORIGIN

For their premium range, Schweppes choose
a formula based on 100% natural sugars and
ingredients from 100% natural sources.

## INGREDIENTS

lavender ...................................................................
orange blossom......................................................
carbonated water..................................................
sugar .......................................................................
citric acid ...............................................................
natural flavourings ..............................................
quinine ...................................................................

## TASTE AND FLAVOUR

Make way for the flavours of the subtly
processed lavender and orange blossom.
The flowery notes completely unfold in
the mouth and give a pleasant hint of the
Mediterranean.

ORIGINAL
PREMIUM MIXER

# 1724
# TONIC WATER

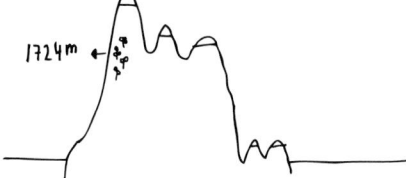

1724m

## ORIGIN

In 2012, creators of Gin Mare brought the tonic 1724 to life. 1724 Tonic Water has been explicitly developed to partner the gin, and you can taste it! To find the essence of the quinine used for 1724 Tonic Water one has to climb high; 1724 metres above sea level to be precise... not a metre higher, not a metre lower! And you guessed it; this is how the name of the tonic came about. The quinine used is found in the Andes, on the so-called Inca trail, and is picked by hand... 1724 Tonic Water is produced in Chile.

## INGREDIENTS

carbonated water ....................................................
natural quinine .......................................................
sugar ......................................................................
infusion of mandarin.............................................

## TASTE AND FLAVOUR

1724 Tonic Water takes you to completely new heights by finding the perfect balance between tradition and originality. The quinine is less bitter because of its Latin American origins. The balanced flavour is peppered with hints of rosemary and thyme. Lightly fruity with an elegant pearly bubble and a note of aniseed in the finish.

# BIG BRANDS

# KINLEY TONIC

## ORIGIN

Kinley Tonic was first introduced into Germany in 1971 by the Coca-Cola Company and is now exported throughout Europe and Asia.

## TASTE AND FLAVOUR

Outspoken bitter tonic taste, with light sweet tones in the background

## INGREDIENTS

sparkling water .......................
sugar ..........................................
citric acid ..................................
flavourings ...............................
quinine .......................................
preservative: potassium sorbate.......................................
antioxidant: ascorbic acid......

# NORDIC MIST
# TONIC WATER

## ORIGIN

Nordic Mist Tonic Water was launched in 1992 by the Coca-Cola Company in New York, Boston, Pittsburgh and Philadelphia.

## TASTE AND FLAVOUR

Nordic Mist has a subdued nose with subtle notes of pine. The bitter taste of quinine is strongly present.

## INGREDIENTS

sparkling water ........................
sugar ...........................................
citric acid ...................................
flavourings .................................
quinine .......................................
sodium benzoate .....................

---

WORLDWIDE

# SCHWEPPES
# INDIAN TONIC

## ORIGIN

Schweppes Indian Tonic is based on the drink the English colonists in India used, a mix of quinine, sugar and bitter orange peel, as a means of preventing malaria. This tonic was first produced by Cadbury Schweppes in London in 1870.

## TASTE AND FLAVOUR

Dry and an early bitter taste

## INGREDIENTS

carbonated water .....................
sugar ...........................................
citric acid ...................................
natural flavouring ....................
quinine flavouring ...................

# THE SENSE OR NONSENSE OF LIGHT TONIC

There are many brands which also offer a light version of their tonics, and those who do not already, are highly likely to follow this trend. And indeed, which soft drink is not available in a light or zero version? Sugars are replaced with artificial sweeteners, fructose or agave syrup, however it goes without saying that artificial sweeteners have been coming under fire for a long time. Stevia, in contrast, purports to be a healthy, or healthier option, but so far there have been no tonics brought to market using it as a sweetener. But it could still happen, and as far as fructose and agave syrup are concerned, we are still sitting on the fence. But why would you choose to mix your gin & tonic using a light tonic? In any event, not for the calorie content, as even the 'fat' version only contains about 35 kcal per 100 ml, so a gin & tonic served in the correct proportions containing around 150 ml tonic amounts to about 53 kcal, as a generous calculation.

So, why bother? Unless you particularly like the taste.

# NOT CONVINCED? MAKE YOUR OWN!

It is also perfectly possible to make your own tonic A quick surf on the net will provide you with a variety of recipes to help you on your way. There is also another alternative: John's Premium® Tonic Syrup. This is the makers' response to, in his opinion, the overly expensive premium tonic waters. The syrup is simply mixed into soda water and you are ready to go: your very own tonic. John makes his syrup with agave, cinchona bark, citric acid, natural oils, and an array of other herbs and spices. Maybe one small minus point is that John's Premium® Tonic Syrup comes all the way from Phoenix, Arizona. After adding up the import costs, it is possibly cheaper to just purchase one of the premium tonics.

# GIN: CATEGORIZATION

SPICY/COMPLEX    CITRUS    SWEET    FLORAL

Historically, we can divide gin into a number of **classic categories:** Old Tom, London Dry, Distilled, Plymouth and Compound gin.

Because of the recent explosion of new gins, today we go further than these classic divisions and make use of the **flavour cross**, with each of the four arms of the cross representing a different taste: **spicy/complex, citrus, sweet** and **floral**. This flavour cross first appeared in 2010 in *IMBIBE*, a leading magazine in the bar community.

In 2010, the palette of tastes didn't take into account the explosive rise of gin, or the creativity of the inventors and distillers. Alongside the completely new generation of gins developed in the last few years, totally new taste experiences have also evolved which can be described as **exotic** thanks to the use of eccentric botanicals. It is not easy to allocate a place on the flavour cross for these gins and for this reason we will be dealing with this category separately.

In this categorization we will also be giving you advice as to which tonic – or which type of tonic – you can best combine with which gin. By now, you know that we can divide tonics into three taste groups: neutral, aromatic and fruity/floral. In other words, for every gin, we will also give the category of the tonic taste, from which you can then choose your favourite. We will also be supporting these descriptions by means of a visual aid, the **G&T flavour cross** (the universe of gins combined with the tonic flavours), so you will be able to clearly see how to make these combinations.

NEUTRAL

FRUITY/ FLORAL

AROMATIC

For now, we will leave the garnish as it is. The priority is to begin with the basics, and for the moment, to concentrate on the facts of the matter, and so the use of a garnish depends on the analysis of the ingredients of your favourite gin & tonic, nothing more and nothing less. But don't worry; we will come back to this in the next chapter, where we relate the theory into practice.

Further on in the book, in the section on the 14 most remarkable gins, we will give you a few complete gin & tonic recipes, including garnish, as inspiration to start you off in making your own creations.

Anyway, let's start at the beginning...

# CLASSIC PRESENTATIONS

## OLD TOM GIN

The name Old Tom gin is used for sweet (retro) gins, like those made during the Gin Craze. This type of gin is rarely used now, but due to the revival of classic cocktails, Old Tom gin is once again being produced, and is becoming more readily available. This gin is sweeter than London Dry and a little dryer than jenever, and so is sometimes referred to as the missing link. The name Old Tom most likely has its origins in the 18th century, when various bars mounted a wooden plaque in the form of a black cat — Old Tom — on the outside walls. Thirsty passers-by could throw a penny into the mouth of the cat and the barman would pour a shot of gin through a small tube which came out between the paws of the cat. And so the first automatic drinks dispenser was born! At the time of writing this book there are around five Old Tom gins on the market. Below are four, and you will find the fifth one further on in the section on aged gins.

Old Tom gins are not combined with tonic, but have recently been brought back onto the market to give bartenders the opportunity to revive retro gin cocktails (such as Tom Collins or Martinez) and get them back on the menu. If you do fancy trying these sweet gins, drink them neat.

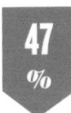

# BOTH'S OLD TOM GIN

### INGREDIENTS

No information available

### COMBINE WITH

drink neat or in
retro cocktails

### ORIGIN

Both's Old Tom Gin is one of the creations
by the German company Haromex. The high
alcohol content of 47% means that this gin is
unique in comparison to other varieties
of Old Tom which only manage a lower
alcohol percentage. The label on the bottle
is made from felt, and is finished with
golden decorative details. The look of the
bottle immediately invokes the glory days
of Old Tom.

### TASTE AND FLAVOUR

Both's has a rather subdued nose, with light
sweet and mild flowery notes. In the mouth
you get a strong fruity sweetness followed by
an intense mix of flowery tones. Strong purple
lavender is conspicuous with a mild flavour
of juniper in the background. Even though
this is a substantial gin, it remains relatively
smooth in the finish.

**40 %**

# HAYMAN'S OLD TOM GIN

## ORIGIN

The Hayman family is one of the oldest distilling families in Great Britain. The Hayman's Old Tom Gin recipe was originally produced between the end of the 19th century and the beginning of the 20th century. Hayman's Old Tom was relaunched in 2007 thanks to increasing demand from bartenders and mixologists who wanted to bring body back to their classic gin cocktails, just like in the 'roaring 20s'. In the 19th century, the family business was taken over by James Burrough, the man who also held the recipe for Beefeater Gin.

## TASTE AND FLAVOUR

Hayman's Old Tom Gin is an intense botanic and lightly sweetened gin which sets it apart from other gins. This gin is used in recipes for numerous classic cocktails such as the Tom Collins or Martinez.

## INGREDIENTS

juniper berry ...........................
coriander seed ........................
angelica .....................................
orange and lemon peel ...........
orris root powder ...................
and others

## COMBINE WITH

drink neat or in
retro cocktails

TOM COLLINS

jensen

jensen's
london
distilled
old
tom
gin

bermondsey gin ltd.,sel 3tq

70cl. e  43%vol.

TD12/164

# 43 %

# JENSEN'S OLD TOM GIN

## ORIGIN

This Old Tom is a product of Christian Jensen who originally wanted to create a London Dry. When visiting Japan, he was given the chance to taste a selection of old gins, some dating as far back as the 40s. The barman responsible for letting him try these gems, challenged Christian to make his own Old Tom style gin. He took a sample to the Thames Distillers and, after trying out many recipes, they developed Jensen's Bermondsey London Dry Gin. Following the success of this gin, Christian once again directed his energies to the challenge, eventually resulting in the creation of Jensen's Old Tom Gin. Old Tom Gin is based on a recipe from the 1840s, in which emphasis is given to a pure palette of tastes, with the juniper playing the leading role. The sweetness of the gin is not created by adding sugar, but instead by liquorice root.

## TASTE AND FLAVOUR

Jensen's Old Tom smells of eucalyptus and juniper berries in combination with liquorice, orange peel and a hint of almond. The tastes are predominantly of eucalyptus, supported by the liquorice. The eucalyptus has a long finish combined with vegetable tints.

## INGREDIENTS

juniper berry...........................
liquorice....................................
eucalyptus ...............................

## COMBINE WITH

drink neat or in retro cocktails

# SECRET TREASURES
## OLD TOM STYLE GIN

### INGREDIENTS

ripe juniper berries from the Apennines and other unlisted herbs and essences

### COMBINE WITH

drink neat or in retro cocktails

### ORIGIN

This gin is part of the Secret Treasures collection, an array of premium spirits from the German company Haromex. Only 700 bottles of this gin are produced per year, making it extremely exclusive. Secret Treasures Old Tom Style Gin was first brought to the market in 2007 and was nominated in the same year at the Berlin Bar Show as 'Spirit of the Year'.

### TASTE AND FLAVOUR

The aroma of Secret Treasures Old Tom Style Gin is sweet and earthy with a weak juniper berry fragrance which fully explodes in the mouth. A dry and fiery mouth feel with a long finish and subtle sweetness.

*The*
**SECRET TREASURES**

## LONDON DRY GIN

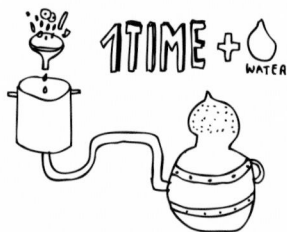

London Dry is a gin with qualitative ingredients, and can be therefore seen as a quality label. London Dry is, in other words, a qualification, signifying a single distillation process during which all the ingredients are distilled together. The only ingredient that may be added after the distillation process is water. London Dry is the classic style of making gin and is not specifically related to the place, and so therefore does not have to come from London per se. London Dry is made in a traditional still, by re-distilling ethyl alcohol together with all the flavourings.

Conditions with which London Dry gin must comply in order to carry the label (EU regulations):

- *The ethyl alcohol must be of high quality. The methanol level in the alcohol may not exceed the maximum of 5 g per hectolitre in 100% alcohol volume.*
- *The flavourings used must be natural, and must only be used to add flavour during the distillation process.*
- *The use of artificial flavourings is forbidden.*
- *The resulting distillate must have a minimum 70% alcohol content.*
- *More ethyl alcohol may be added after distillation, but it must be of the same quality.*
- *The distillate may be sweetened as long as the sugars do not exceed the maximum level of 0.5 g per litre in the final product.*
- *The only other ingredient that may be added after distillation is water.*
- *In no instance may London Dry be coloured.*

### DISTILLED GIN

Distilled gin is characterized by the same process as London Dry, but extra infusions may be added after, or extra ingredients added during, the distillation process. Many of the 'premium gins' fall into this category.

### COMPOUND GIN

Compound gin mostly consists of a few added flavourings and extracts, often with no actual distillation of botanicals at all. Frequently all that is mentioned on the label is that it is gin. Mostly supermarket or liquor traders own brands are compound gins.

### PLYMOUTH GIN

Plymouth Gin is a one of a kind gin, produced by the Black Friars Distillery inside the walls of what was once a Dominican monastery in the city of, you guessed it, Plymouth. Plymouth Gin gained popularity at the beginning of the 20th century and also has protected geographical indication, which relates to all gins distilled in Plymouth. To this day, there is only one brand of gin with this distinction: Plymouth Gin.

Plymouth Gin should be combined with a neutral tonic.

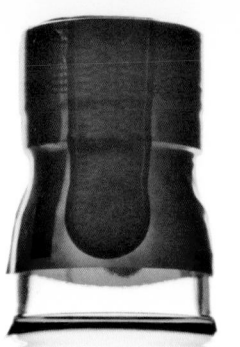

PLYMOUTH GIN

TRADE MARK

IN 1620 THE MAYFLOWER SET
SAIL FROM PLYMOUTH ON
A JOURNEY OF HOPE
AND DISCOVERY

41.2% Vol.   BATCH DISTILLED IN THE ORIGINAL   70cle
VICTORIAN COPPER STILL

Black Friars Distillery

PROTECTED STATUS

COATES & Co

BLACK FRIARS
DISTILLERY

# PLYMOUTH GIN

**41,2 %**

## ORIGIN

In 1793, in an old Dominican monastery, Fox and Williamson began distilling the brand, Plymouth. Soon after, Fox & Williamson became known as Coates & Co, and so they remained until March 2004. In 2005, the brand was bought by the Swedish V&S Group. Now however (since 2008), it is owned by the French company Pernod Ricard. The first bottle of Plymouth Gin depicted a monk on the inside of the back label. In 2006, the form of the bottle changed to become more art deco in style with a picture of The Mayflower ship on the front. In 2012, Plymouth Gin once again changed its look, going back to basics with a more classic shaped bottle with green tinted glass. Plymouth Gin is distilled using a unique combination of at least seven different botanical herbs and spices and pure grain alcohol. Between 1999 and 2006, Plymouth Gin took home various awards, from amongst others 'International Spirits Challenge', 'Beverage Testing Institute', 'The International Wine and Spirits Competition' and the 'San Francisco World Spirits Competition'.

## TASTE AND FLAVOUR

The aroma of the juniper is clearly present, but is also supported by lavender, camphor, lemon, sage and eucalyptus. The taste is fresh with hints of lemon and orange. The character of this gin is shaped by the subtle addition of coriander and white pepper corns.

## INGREDIENTS

juniper berry.............................
cardamom..................................
orris root...................................
coriander ..................................
lemon and orange peel ..........

## COMBINE WITH

neutral tonic or
classic cocktails

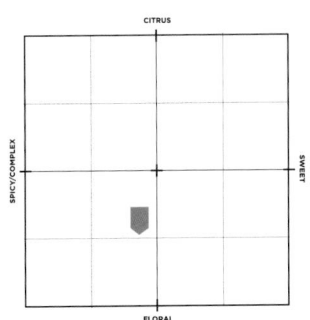

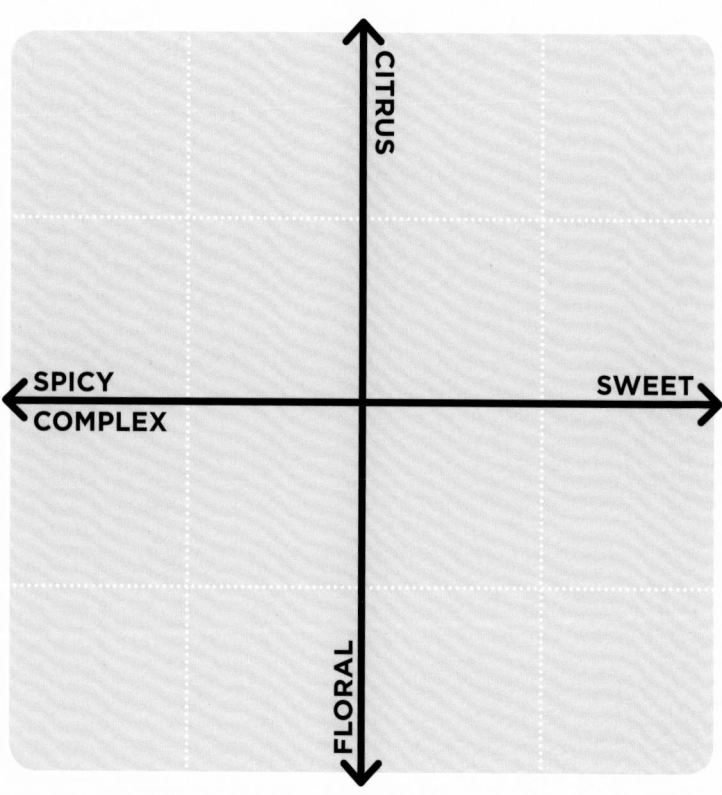

CITRUS

SPICY
COMPLEX

SWEET

FLORAL

# CLASSIFICATION ACCORDING TO THE FLAVOUR CROSS

To properly demonstrate the use of the flavour cross we will take a few ambassadors from the new generation of gins and give them a place on the first version of the cross.

Please note: this is not to say that the old guard, like for example Bombay Sapphire, Beefeater Gin, Gordon's Gin, etc., do not warrant a place on the flavour cross. The typical London Dry gins find themselves close to the centre because of their classic gin flavour.

Since we don't want to leave anyone 'thirsty' for too long, we also give the tonics a place on the flavour cross. In this second version, we clarify straight away which tonic should be combined with which gin.

In principal a neutral tonic can be mixed with any gin, however they really come into their own in the centre of the flavour cross with the classic London Dry flavours.

First we will concentrate on the term New Western gin or New Generation gin.

## NEW WESTERN GIN
## OR NEW GENERATION GIN

The new generation of gins date their renaissance from the year 2000 onwards, and have a herby and balanced aroma alongside the dominant juniper berry. The term New Western gin was conceived by Ryan Magarian, an internationally acclaimed bartender from the USA and co-creator of Aviation Gin. The term New Western gin has in the meantime become ingrained in the world of mixology. As authors of this book we also include the previous generation of gins under the heading New Generation gin. Why? The only reason is to make it easier and clearer for you. Are you a professional? Well then you are undoubtedly already familiar with the term New Western gin and you can safely skip over the following comments.

New Western gins stem from the efforts of both big brand producers and regional distilleries and gin adepts. By adepts we mean those passionate believers who knock on the doors of distilleries to get their own gin developed. After casting an eye over the available range of dry gins, they all saw that there was huge potential in creating new gins with more 'freedom of taste'; thus, an opportunity to put other botanicals into the spotlight alongside the juniper berry, which had had the starring role for so many years. Legally speaking the juniper berry has to remain the dominant flavour, but this new generation is not only defined by juniper but also by the careful integration of other supporting flavours.

According to Ryan Magarian, Tanqueray Malacca is one of the first New Western gins ever created. First introduced in 1997, this gin label was quickly taken off the market in 2001 due to limited success. It is possible that ten years ago, the timing was just not right for the new evolution in gin, or perhaps it's better to call it a gin revolution. Today however, it is a different story. In 2013, the label was brought back for the general public and has proved to be a big success. Hendrick's Gin followed suit and brought out a gin with aromas of cucumber and Bulgarian rose. This opened the floodgates, leading to other new artisan gins, only too happy to show off their creativity and regional specialities. The number of New Western gins on offer is on the rise, and keeps rising to this day.

BULGARIAN ROSE

HENDRICK'S GIN

CUCUMBER

## THE FLAVOUR CROSS AND SOME GIN AMBASSADORS

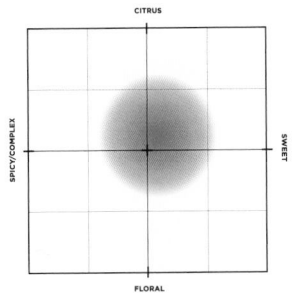

### IN THE MIDDLE:
### CLASSIC LONDON DRY STYLE
COMBINE WITH NEUTRAL TONIC

As mentioned earlier, London Dry is a classic style of creating gin and is a label of quality, which furthermore has nothing to do with the place it is made or the taste of the gin.

It is true that London Dry was (before the 'gin explosion' of the last few years) considered to be the typical gin taste: sharp bitter (sweet), a hint of citrus and a dry finish. Nowadays, gins which carry the label London Dry have very little in common with the Dry gins of the past.

One thing is certain though, to be allowed to carry the label London Dry, the gin must conform to certain EU regulations and conditions (see page 80). There are also many new gins which comply with these regulations, and so likewise belong in this category. These comply with the rules of what a London Dry should be, but introduce new botanicals and distillation techniques, moving further and further away from the centre of the flavour cross. To sum up: a gin that finds itself close to the centre has the classical London Dry taste. The further away it deviates from the centre of the cross, the more different the taste notes are, or to say it in another way, the more the citrus-sweet-floral-spicy/complex taste manifest themselves in the gin.

# BEEFEATER GIN

## ORIGIN

Beefeater is owned by Pernod Ricard and bottled and distributed by James Burrough Ltd. Beefeater was owned by the Burrough family up until 1987. Named after the 'Yeomen Warders' better known as 'Beefeaters': the ceremonial guards at the Tower of London. A unique feature of Beefeater Gin's production is that the peel from lemons and oranges, the entire juniper berries and other plant botanicals are allowed to steep for 24 hours before they are distilled. This process ensures that the aromas are completely extracted. The distillation itself takes about eight hours and the whole process is closely watched over by master distiller Desmond Payne.

## TASTE AND FLAVOUR

One of the classics, and the most recognisable, typical London Dry on the market. On the nose, juniper, black pepper and orange. Beefeater Gin has a sharp and dry taste. On the palate, an explosion of citrus and juniper berry in the finish.

## INGREDIENTS

juniper berry ..............................
angelica .......................................
angelica seed .............................
coriander seed ..........................
liquorice root ...........................
almonds.......................................
orris root ....................................
Seville oranges..........................
lemon peel ................................

## COMBINE WITH

neutral tonic

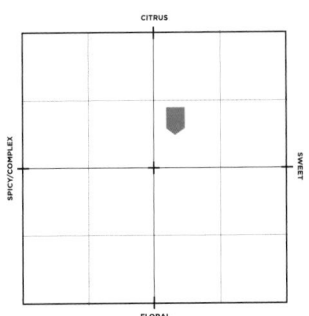

# GREENALL'S LONDON DRY GIN

## ORIGIN

Greenall's London Dry Gin was first developed in 1761. Since then, little has changed from the original family recipe. The gin has been distilled in Warrington for the past 250 years. This distillery was set up by Thomas Dakin who, in 1860, sold it to the Greenall family. The craft and expertise of the Greenall family has been passed from generation to generation and today sees the seventh master distiller, Joanne Moore, carefully watching over the quality of Greenall's Gin.

## TASTE AND FLAVOUR

A fresh and inspirational gin with hints of juniper berry and citrus fruit in the mouth. A traditional London Dry, well-balanced with a nicely rounded flavour that is not too complex.

## INGREDIENTS

No information available

## COMBINE WITH

neutral tonic

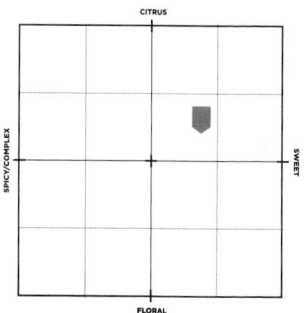

Greenall's

# SIPSMITH GIN

## ORIGIN

Sipsmith Independent Distillers was set up in London in 2009. After years of gaining experience in the drinks industry, a group of friends made the decision to go into business to brew their own gin and follow their passion for artisan spirits. They call themselves 'sip-smiths'. The smiths still make use of the traditional production processes, the so-called 'one-shot' gin. In this process the botanicals are distilled with the spirit, and the herbs are only used once for one batch only. Aside from the ingredients, this is a really unique London Dry Gin due to the use of vodka as the base for the production. Sipsmith Gin has taken home many awards due to its taste and craftsmanship.

## TASTE AND FLAVOUR

On the nose, the flowery tints are reminiscent of summer meadows, filled out with the round fragrance of the juniper berry and the freshness of citrus. Tastes of juniper, lemon tart, and orange marmalade are recognisable in this gin. Sipsmith Gin finishes like any classic London Dry: dry with hints of juniper and lemon.

## INGREDIENTS

juniper berry.............................
Seville orange ..........................
Spanish lemon peel ................
Bulgarian coriander seed .......
French angelica .......................
Spanish liquorice root ...........
Italian orris root......................
cinnamon from Madagascar..
Chinese cassia bark ................
ground almonds
from Spain ................................

## COMBINE WITH

neutral tonic

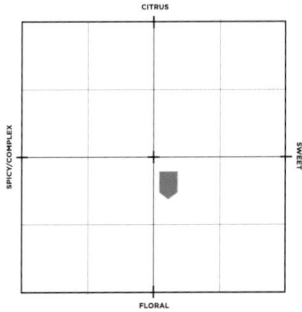

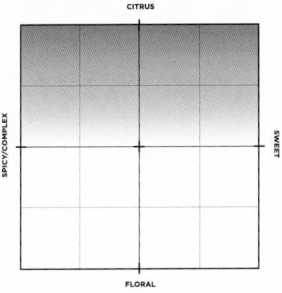

## ON THE TOP: CITRUS
### COMBINE WITH AROMATIC TONIC
### (OR NEUTRAL TONIC)

The gins situated at the top of the flavour cross have an outspoken citrus taste: spicy, sour tones such as bergamot (bitter orange), grapefruit, orange, lemon and lime. This is not to say that you will necessarily find these flavours present, as you will often discover other very different taste accents, but the master distillers or creators of these kinds of gin are certainly of the opinion that citrus is a very important, and above all, delicious ingredient. In summary: the name 'citrus' is a collective name for a mishmash of all sorts of fruit with a peel, meaning you can discover a vast difference from (citrus)gin to (citrus)gin, in this corner of the flavour cross. Something else worthy of note: these gins always offer a certain freshness, especially in a gin & tonic, so come highly recommended for a warm summer's day...

**LONDON DISTILLED
DRY GIN**

70cl.   ALC. 47% BY VOL.

# HASWELL GIN

### ORIGIN

Haswell London Dry Gin is an award-winning gin, created by Julian Haswell. According to Julian, the three most important ingredients of a classic London Dry gin are the juniper berry, angelica and coriander seed. On this basis Julian creates a gin with the unashamedly citrus flavours of sweet and bitter oranges with just a touch of lemon.

### TASTE AND FLAVOUR

The powerful citrus flavours of oranges with a hint of lemon

### INGREDIENTS

juniper berry ............................
angelica ......................................
coriander seed .........................
savoury ......................................
lime peel from Spain ..............
Aframomum melegueta or grains of paradise (a peppery spice from West Africa) ................
bitter orange peel from Morocco and Haiti..................
sweet orange peel from Morocco and Spain........
liquorice root ...........................

### COMBINE WITH

aromatic tonic
(or neutral tonic)

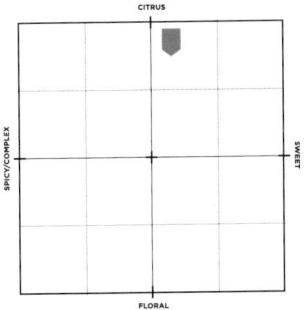

# LONDON N°3

**46 %**

## ORIGIN

Despite the British roots of this gin, it is actually distilled in the Netherlands by de Kuyper Royal Distillers. De Kuyper is a 100% family-owned business and is the world's largest producer of cocktail liqueurs. De Kuyper was granted permission to produce London N°3 which is based on a recipe from Berry Bros. & Rudd, London's oldest wine and spirits merchants. Named N°3 after the address in St. James Street in London where the wine and spirit merchants have been based since 1698. With juniper berry as its base, this gin is an ode to the integrity and character of a traditional London Dry Gin. Six perfectly balanced botanicals are distilled in traditional copper pot stills.

## TASTE AND FLAVOUR

Because London N°3 is flavoured with three types of spice and three types of fruit, it is perfectly balanced. There are fresh aromas of grapefruit and orange, and a recognisable scent of cardamom. The taste can be perfectly attributed to the use of grapefruit, which is supported by the spicy coriander. An earthy dryness comes through in the finish.

## INGREDIENTS

juniper berry from Italy .........
Spanish orange peel ...............
grapefruit...................................
angelica ......................................
Moroccan coriander seed ......
cardamom...................................

## COMBINE WITH

aromatic tonic
(or neutral tonic)

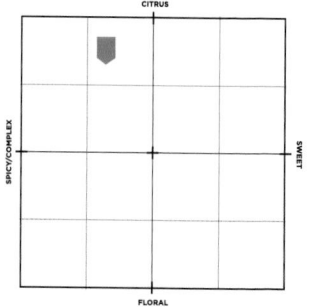

CITRUS

SPICY/COMPLEX

SWEET

FLORAL

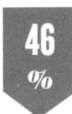

# N°209

**46 %**

## ORIGIN

N°209 is a prestigious, artisan premium gin from San Francisco. The name is due to the fact that this was the 209th distillery registered in the United States. N°209 gin came into being thanks to Leslie Rudd. Leslie was a winemaker producing exclusive wines at his vineyard in the Napa Valley. The distiller, avid amateur cook and saxophonist, Arne Hillesland's creative spirit and love of cuisine proved to be the ideal combination to blend with Leslie's wine expertise. The result is a top quality gin that is soft and memorable.

## TASTE AND FLAVOUR

N°209 opens with an aromatic nose of citrus and floral tones with a hint of spiciness. The palette of flavours begins with the high notes of lemon and lime followed by orange. As the gin warms in the mouth, the flowery tones of the coriander and Bergamot are released. This is subtly followed by the warmth of pepper from the cardamom and juniper berry. A surprising twist comes when the 'mint components' of the cardamom are released. N°209 ends with the cassia bark in the finish.

## INGREDIENTS

juniper berry.............................
angelica ....................................
lemon peel ...............................
Bergamot orange peel.............
coriander .................................
cardamom.................................
cassia bark ...............................

## COMBINE WITH

aromatic tonic
(or neutral tonic)

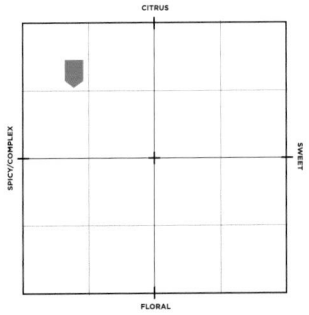

**41,3 %**

# TANQUERAY RANGPUR GIN

## ORIGIN

Tanqueray Rangpur Gin was launched in 2006 and perfectly completes the Tanqueray brand range. This gin is part of the new generation which sets itself apart, thanks to the flavouring of Rangpur fruit (a cross between mandarin and lemon) from India.

## TASTE AND FLAVOUR

The fragrance of sweet citrus and the soft bouquet of roses invites a long, slow swallow. The botanic aromas greet the tongue subtly and continue through to peak at juniper berry, rounding off with citrus.

## INGREDIENTS

juniper berry.............................
Rangpur fruit...........................
coriander .................................
bay leaf ...................................
ginger.......................................

## COMBINE WITH

aromatic tonic
(or neutral tonic)

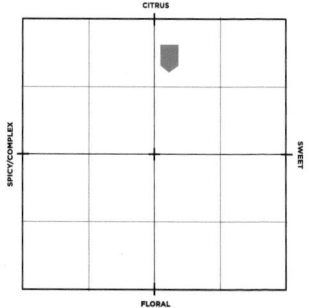

# Tanqueray

EXPORT STRENGT

# ANGPU

...CED AND BOTTLED IN GREAT...
...OR CHARLES TANQUERAY &...

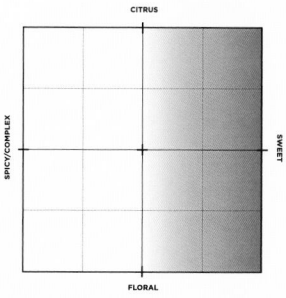

## ON THE RIGHT: SWEET
### COMBINE WITH FRUITY TONIC
### (OR NEUTRAL TONIC)

Gins with a distinctly sweet taste can also include the retro Old Tom gins, whereby extra natural sugars are added, as well as Dry gins where sweet botanicals dominate. Liquorice root is a key ingredient in this case. Liquorice is so to speak the 'candy cane' of the master distiller. The amount of liquorice used will by and large determine whether a gin will tend toward this taste direction.

BATCH N° 21/12

## *Fifty Pounds*

### GIN

RARE *and* HANDCRAFTED
LONDON DRY GIN

*Distilled in London*

ORIGINAL RECIPE

# FIFTY POUNDS GIN

**43,5 %**

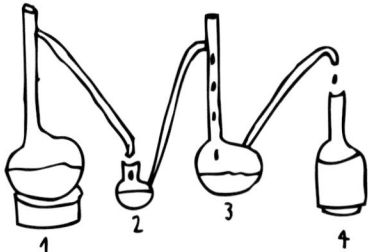

1    2    3    4

## ORIGIN

Fifty Pounds Gin is produced in a small distillery in South East London. This extremely soft London Dry owes its name to the 'tax rise' levied during the time of the Gin Act in 1736. Fifty Pounds is made using traditional methods and uses exclusively natural ingredients. The neutral alcohol is obtained by a fourfold distillation of the wheat. The alcohol is then distilled once again, this time with the addition of herbs and botanicals from all over the world.

## TASTE AND FLAVOUR

Fifty Pounds Gin has a heady bouquet, full of citrus, mint, lavender and juniper berry. On tasting, it is mostly the aniseed and pepper flavours that come to the foreground. The coriander seed helps accentuate the sweet taste.

## INGREDIENTS

juniper berry from Croatia ....
coriander seed from
the Middle East .......................
grains of paradise from
the Gulf of Guinea ...................
savoury from the
South of France .......................
orange and lemon peel
from Spain ................................
liquorice from Calabria ..........
angelica from
Western Europe ......................
Other ingredients are also
used, but that secret stays
in South East London.

## COMBINE WITH

fruity tonic
(or neutral tonic)

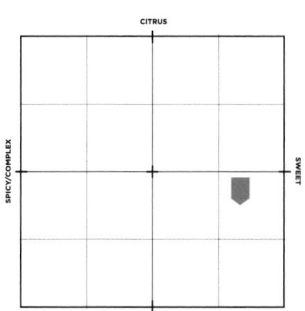

# OLD ENGLISH GIN

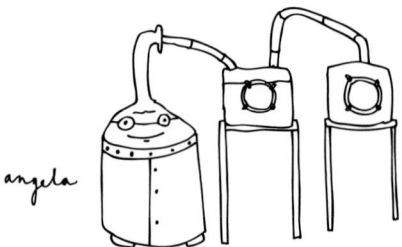

*angela*

## ORIGIN

This gin is made following a recipe from 1783 and continues to be distilled in the oldest pot still in England by the Langley Distillers. The boiler is called Angela or Grandma, after the grandmother of the original distiller. This gin is uniquely bottled in 100% recycled old champagne bottles. Old English Gin was launched in 2012.

## TASTE AND FLAVOUR

From the moment you pop the cork you are rewarded with the fresh aroma of juniper berries. This fragrance is quickly followed by a rich earthy complexity of warm hay, black pepper and spices. In the background, hints of basil and mint. The taste is surprising due to the controlled sweetness and a silky soft mouth feel.

## INGREDIENTS

juniper berry ..............................
coriander ...................................
lemon and orange peel ...........
angelica .....................................
orris root ...................................
cassia ..........................................
cinnamon ...................................
liquorice ....................................
nutmeg .......................................
cardamom ...................................

## COMBINE WITH

fruity tonic
(or neutral tonic)

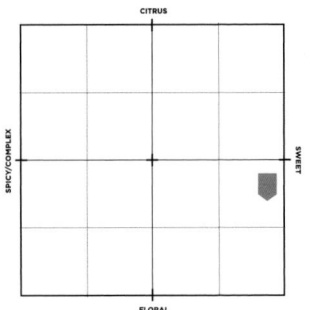

PURE OLD POT STILL

HAMMER
& SON
LTD.

AD ORIGINEM 1783

Old English

DISTILLED AND BOTTLED IN ENGLAND

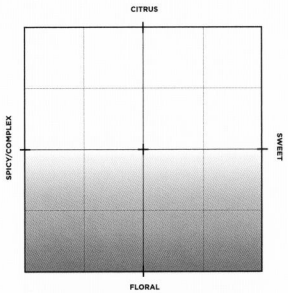

## AT THE BOTTOM: FLORAL
### COMBINE WITH FRUITY TONIC
### (OR NEUTRAL TONIC)

Gins which inhabit the bottom arm of the flavour cross are notably floral in character. Summery tastes such as elderflower and honeysuckle are clearly present. The floral tints appear thanks to the use of an assortment of flower-like products (editor's note: not the most obvious botanicals to begin with) and tea extracts. This corner of the flavour cross is where the gins with predominantly fruity tones can be located.

**44 %**

# CITADELLE GIN

## ORIGIN

Citadelle Gin is originally a French gin with 19 different herbal ingredients, distilled three times. The brand was first brought to market in 1998 and is produced in Cognac by Gabriel & Andreu. Citadelle is distributed by Cognac-Ferrand and is named after an 18th century distillery in Dunkirk. This gin has won countless awards, far too many to list here. No expense has been spared for the botanicals, with a seemingly worldwide hunt to gather this treasure trove of spices.

## TASTE AND FLAVOUR

The taste is unusual in comparison with other gins, due to its pleasant and aromatic character, amidst beautiful undertones of fresh flowers, jasmine, honeysuckle and cinnamon. It is a gin with an unusually broad spectrum of flavours, but little else is expected from 19 different botanicals. The longer the gin stays in the mouth, the more the palette of flavours changes in character, and the ingredients such as the aniseed, grain and cinnamon come to the fore. A lively gin with a distinctly floral character.

## INGREDIENTS

juniper berry from France .....
Moroccan coriander...............
orange peel from Mexico .......
cardamom from India............
liquorice from China..............
cubeb pepper from Java .........
French flavourings..................
Mediterranean fennel............
Italian orris root.....................
cinnamon from Sri Lanka ......
French violets .........................
almonds from Spain ...............
cassia from Indochina ...........
German angelica .....................
grains of paradise from
West Africa...............................
Dutch cumin ...........................
nutmeg from India ..................
Spanish lemons .......................
star anise from France ...........

## COMBINE WITH

fruity tonic (or neutral tonic)

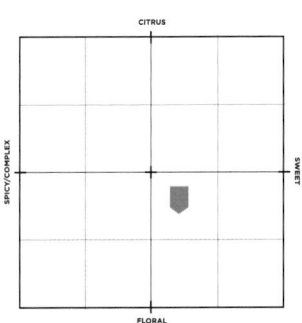

# GERANIUM GIN

**44 %**

## INGREDIENTS

juniper berry...........................
oil of the Danish
geranium plant........................
coriander ..................................
lemon peel ...............................
angelica ....................................
orris root...................................
aniseed .....................................
cinnamon..................................
and other unnamed
ingredients

## COMBINE WITH

fruity tonic
(or neutral tonic)

## ORIGIN

Geranium Gin is a creation by a father-son team looking for the perfect gin. Dane Henrik Hammer and his father have crafted a gin that is both dry and floral in flavour. This London Dry gin combines juniper berry with the oil of Danish geranium plants. This Geranium Gin is distilled in the traditional way but with the addition of a few new techniques. Henrik's father, a chemist by trade, has succeeded in extracting the oils from the geranium plant, and we can see — or rather drink — the results.

## TASTE AND FLAVOUR

Geranium Gin has a slightly spicy and a definite floral taste, held up by the London Dry character.

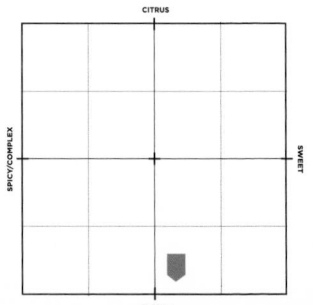

*Geranium*

*Premium
London Dry Gin*

*by Hammer & Son*

# hernö

swedish excellenc

# HERNÖ SWEDISH EXCELLENCE GIN

## ORIGIN

Hernö Gin comes from the most northerly distillery in the world, situated in the north of Sweden, in Dala. The gin is distilled in a German-made, hand-beaten copper boiler, which can hold 250 litres. The copper boiler is named 'Kierstin' and was fitted in 2012. The complete production process is artisanal and only natural botanicals and homemade grain alcohol is used. The eight botanicals macerate for at least 18 hours in the grain alcohol before the distillation process begins. This is a gin with a distinct personality, reflecting the individuality of the distillery and the master distiller.

## TASTE AND FLAVOUR

The taste begins with juniper berry, before revealing a jam-like combination of flowery aromas. The finish is long and lingering, with plenty of citrus and nuttiness thanks to the use of almond and nutmeg.

## INGREDIENTS

juniper berry.............................
coriander ...................................
meadowsweet...........................
cassia.........................................
black pepper ............................
vanilla .......................................
lingonberry..............................
lemon peel ...............................

## COMBINE WITH

fruity tonic (or neutral tonic)

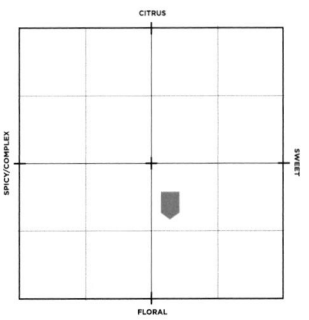

# NOLET'S DRY GIN

**47,6 %**

## ORIGIN

In 1691, Joannes Nolet set up his distillery in the Dutch town of Schiedam. He chose the location as it was close to the North Sea and the big grain auctions. The Nolet Distillery in Schiedam has now been producing high quality spirits for ten generations. It is the oldest surviving distillery in the Netherlands which is still owned by the family who started it. Nolet's Silver Dry Gin uses a distinctive combination of botanicals never before used in gin, such as Turkish rose, peach and raspberry. The basis of the gin is distilled in pot stills. The extracts of the roses, peaches and raspberries are distilled separately and then combined with the juniper base. Afterwards, the blend is allowed to rest so as to reach the perfect balance.

## TASTE AND FLAVOUR

This ultra-premium gin is a good example of a fruity-floral gin with the aromas of roses, peaches and blackberry. The taste is, at the very least, surprising for a gin and deviates from the traditional juniper berry. Despite the high alcohol content, this gin is very soft.

## INGREDIENTS

juniper berry............................
wheat.........................................
lime ...........................................
orris root ...................................
liquorice ....................................
peaches......................................
raspberries.................................
Turkish roses ...........................

## COMBINE WITH

fruity tonic
(or neutral tonic)

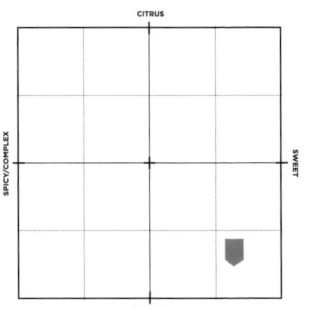

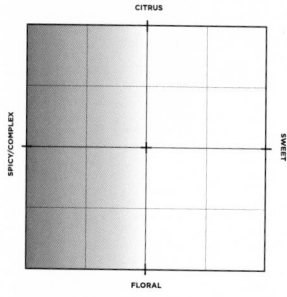

## ON THE LEFT: SPICY/COMPLEX
COMBINE WITH AROMATIC TONIC
(OR NEUTRAL TONIC)

Complex flavours and spicy tones predominate. Think of earthy tastes, pepper and hints of herbs and spices, such as fennel and ginger, but also chocolate, apples and wood. Gins which find themselves in this corner of our taste spectrum are a real joyride for the gin lover. Whereas in the other corners of our flavour cross we can speak of monotone flavours — and that is certainly not to say 'boring', but more a sign of quality of content — with this type of gin the drinker will enjoy a roller-coaster ride of taste impressions. When trying a spicy/complex gin neat, you will discover that the first, typical flavours of gin are often next replaced by new nuances in the body of the drink. On the finish, even more taste sensations come peeping around the corner. It is precisely this multifaceted nature which acts as the power (and definition) behind complex gins. And yes indeed, we are getting more daring by choosing these kinds of gin more regularly. The adventurous type always does prefer the roller-coaster at the funfair. Would you rather play it safe? In that case, it is perhaps wise to leave this area of the flavour cross well alone.

®

Reisetbauer

# BLUE GIN

PREMIUM
AUSTRIAN
QUALITY
VINTAGE
DISTILLED
**DRY GIN**
SMALL BATCH

43% VOL ℮ 70CL

# BLUE GIN

## ORIGIN

Blue Gin is from the hands of the Austrian distillers Hans Reisetbauer, who brought this surprising gin to the market place in 2006. The distillation process is unusual to say the least. Small copper boilers, each with a 300-litre capacity, are used to first distill the raw materials such as the grain type 'Mulan' and corn, using the 'pot still' method with a basic distillate of 40% alcohol. The second distillation uses 96% alcohol and more than 27 botanicals sourced from no less than ten different countries such as Spain, Vietnam, Egypt, Romania, China, Indonesia, The Netherlands, Turkey and America. During the three day fermentation period, the mixture is processed again using the pot still method, followed by splitting the botanicals and the alcohol. Blue Gin is then diluted with crystal clear water from the 'Alm' mountain river.

## TASTE AND FLAVOUR

The flavour is fresh, elegant and spicy, with the typical tastes of juniper berry filled out with hints of citrus. The spicy finish with its surprising earthy taste certainly makes this a gin worth investigating.

## INGREDIENTS

juniper berry.............................
grated lemon peel ...................
angelica .....................................
coriander seed .........................
turmeric ....................................
liquorice....................................
and others

## COMBINE WITH

aromatic tonic
(or neutral tonic)

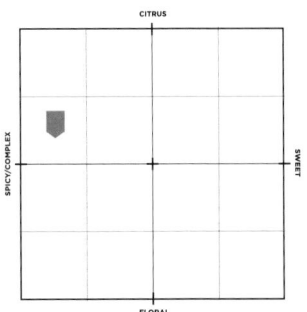

# BULLDOG GIN

40%

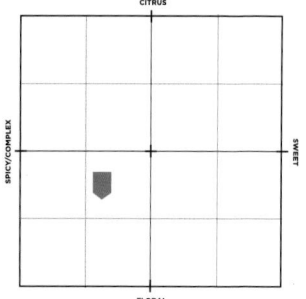

## ORIGIN

A really butch gin from London, launched in 2007 by a former investment banker. The twelve botanicals in the gin represent the brand's worldwide trip. The bottle has a rugged-looking studded dog collar illustrating its domineering character. The gin is distilled four times and has received worldwide acclaim. Bulldog Gin is perfect to drink 'on the rocks', but can also hold its own in any number of cocktails.

## TASTE AND FLAVOUR

Once you have dared to open the bottle, the very flowery bouquet of coriander and citrus becomes immediately apparent. Very dry and soft on the palate, where the juniper plays a dominant role. Bulldog Gin is brought into balance by the botanical elements.

## INGREDIENTS

juniper berry.............................
almonds.....................................
lavender ....................................
cassia bark ................................
coriander seed .........................
dragon eye (a type of lychee) ......
liquorice...................................
poppy.........................................
lotus leaves ..............................

## COMBINE WITH

aromatic tonic
(or neutral tonic)

CITRUS

SPICY/COMPLEX

SWEET

FLORAL

**BULLDOG**

A Brazen B...
Perfectly B...
Natural Pour...
And Hint...
Bulldog Gu...
Tra...
Meet...
R...

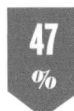

# MONKEY 47

## ORIGIN

Monkey 47 is a complex, full-flavoured gin from the Black Forest. The name gives you a clue as to both the number of botanicals used (47), as well as the alcohol content (47%). Before bottling, Monkey 47 is left to mature for about 100 days in earthenware vats. The label marks not only the date of bottling, but also the vat and bottle number. The character of Monkey 47 is determined by the traditional British recipe, combined with botanicals from the Black Forest and India. Today, this gin is produced by Black Forest Distillers.

## TASTE AND FLAVOUR

Monkey 47 is a highly unusual gin with a clean flavour. The taste of the juniper berry and citrus is complemented by sweet and floral aromas, giving the gin a spicy 'bite'. Peppery spices and bitter fruits complete the picture.

### INGREDIENTS

47 botanicals including
juniper berry............................
cranberries ...............................
pine needles .............................
lavender ....................................
pepper .......................................
cloves.........................................
Approximately 23 of the botanicals originate from the Black Forest.

### COMBINE WITH

aromatic tonic
(or neutral tonic)

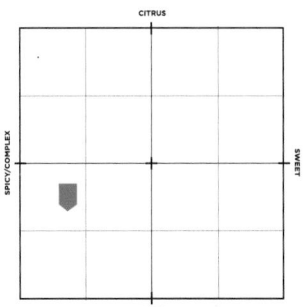

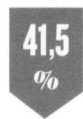

# MOMBASA CLUB GIN

**41,5 %**

## ORIGIN

Mombasa Club Gin is an archetypal retro gin, made following a 19th century recipe which was originally intended for the British colonists in Mombasa (Kenya). These colonists founded the first exclusive club — you guessed it — the legendary Mombasa Club. Some of the Mombasa Club members — naturally only English — were privileged enough to enjoy this gin. Nowadays, this spirit is crafted from carefully selected aromatic herbs and spices and new life has been breathed into the authentic flavours of this exclusive recipe.

## TASTE AND FLAVOUR

Mombasa Club Gin smells exotic and tastes sweet but, at the same time, fresh. In one word: elegant. Overall it is pretty spicy, and the lime and aniseed tints contribute to the complete package. The finish is an elongated bitterness. Mombasa Club Gin lends itself wonderfully to being served 'on the rocks'.

## INGREDIENTS

juniper berry.............................
cassia bark ...............................
cumin........................................
coriander .................................
cloves.......................................
exotic angelica..........................
and others

## COMBINE WITH

aromatic tonic
(or neutral tonic)

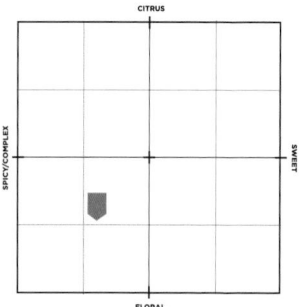

# EXOTIC GINS

The flavour cross is our guide to the categorization of gins. Due to recent developments in flavours, there are some gins that we cannot equivocally place on the flavour cross. Therefore we define these gins as exotic. Just as a few years ago in the world of whisky, the producers shifted the boundaries with regards to taste, and so completely new taste experiences are also manifesting in the gin universe.

Let's give you an example to clarify. The word 'finishers' has recently started popping up in connection with whisky. Big brands have been trying to maintain the perception of whisky as a sexy product by offering new patterns of taste. Instead of maturing the whisky in classic wooden barrels, the producers are now also making use of old wine vats, old port vats or old Madeira vats. This leads to totally new flavour variations. The same phenomenon is also occurring with gin. Producers are breaking through the so called 'flavour boundary' and are experimenting with new ingredients and working methods. So for instance, Hoxton Gin uses coconut as an ingredient and Gin Mare, amongst others, creatively uses Arbequina olives. New methods of finishing are being established, with some gins left to mature in vats, such as Ransom Old Tom Gin, Columbian Aged Gin and Citadelle Réserve Gin.

In support of our convictions we will be discussing some of the exotic gins on the basis of their ingredients. Aged gins will come later and have a place in our section on mavericks.

At this exotic level of gins, our tonic categorization as we discussed earlier is not applicable, and therefore it is necessary to assess each gin individually.

MEDITERRANEAN GIN
*Colección de autor.*

GIN MARE

DISTILLED FROM OLIVES, THYME, ROSEMARY AND BASIL

700 mL   Alc. 42,7 % vol.

**42,7 %**

# GIN MARE

## ORIGIN

Gin Mare is made with the highest quality botanical herbs and spices, predominantly selected from the Mediterranean region. These are separately distilled in Vilanova i la Geltrú, a village on the Costa Dorada — and just to it make even more idyllic — in a picturesque old chapel. The domain is a former refuge for monks. In 1950, the terrain was purchased by the Giro Ribot family to accommodate their growing business. Launched in 1940, their MG Gin was a big hit in Spain. Later, in 2007, they made the decision to join Global Premium Brands — who had much more marketing experience than the Ribot brothers — and began developing a new gin. Gin Mare came to light in 2008 after much experimentation with a variety of herbs and spices. In 2012, the brand launched a new bottle.

## TASTE AND FLAVOUR

A herby nose, reminiscent of a damp forest full of tomato plants, alongside subtle aromas of rosemary and black olives. A full taste which bursts open with the juniper berries and coriander before switching over to the bitter, herby tones of thyme, rosemary and basil. The light bitter finish has notes of green olive, cardamom and basil. This super-premium gin has a character all of its own and a balance that is unlike any other gin on the market.

## INGREDIENTS

hand-picked juniper berry.....
Arbequina olives ......................
rosemary from Greece............
Italian basil..............................
Turkish thyme ........................
coriander from Morocco........
cardamom from Sri Lanka.....
bitter oranges from Seville ....
sweet oranges
from Valencia...........................
lemons from Lleida ................

## COMBINE WITH

1724 Tonic Water or Fever-Tree Mediterranean Tonic Water

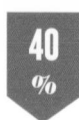

# GIN SEA

18 90

## ORIGIN

Gin Sea is owned by one of the most famous sommeliers in Spain, Manuel Barrientos, but it was a collaboration of more than 100 professionals who developed the recipe. Gin Sea uses a 100% grain distillate from London which has been distilled five times. Ten different botanicals are used for the formula. Each ingredient is steeped separately and then distilled in an old still from Herve & Moulin (Bordeaux), which has been in service since 1890. Hence the reference to 1890 on the label.

## TASTE AND FLAVOUR

Delicate flavours with a touch of spice. Pleasantly fresh from the mint. In turn, the citrus in turn ensures a certain crispness.

## INGREDIENTS

juniper berry...........................
cardamom.................................
coriander ..................................
thyme.......................................
bitter chamomile......................
liquorice ..................................
peppermint...............................
lemon peel ...............................
the peel of sweet and
bitter oranges..........................

## COMBINE WITH

Thomas Henry Tonic

# G'VINE FLORAISON

**40 %**

## ORIGIN

G'Vine Gin is produced by EuroWineGate, a French company set up in 2001 and located in the Cognac region of France. The founders are 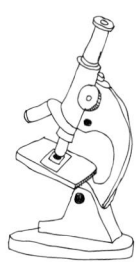 oenologists and have 45 years of collective knowhow in the production and selling of wines and spirits. A daring ultra-premium gin based on the highly prized Ugni Blanc grape, this gin bridges the gap between a flavoured vodka and gin. Floraison is French for blossom time: when the fruit on the grapevines is just starting to grow (setting) which takes place once a year in mid-June. G'Vine Gin has also won many awards.

## TASTE AND FLAVOUR

The taste of G'Vine is soft with an undertone of flowers and grass. The spectrum of flavours in G'Vine is broad: velvety, full, soft and exuberant spice, strong, intense and audacious. We get an alcohol which is softer and stronger than a classic grain-based gin. Amongst the palette of flavours of the other aromatic plants is also the soft note of vine blossom.

## INGREDIENTS

juniper berry...........................
Ugni Blanc grape.....................
coriander .................................
pepper berries ........................
ginger........................................
liquorice...................................
cardamom................................
cassia........................................
lime ..........................................

## COMBINE WITH

1724 Tonic Water or
Fever-Tree Tonic

# SAFFRON GIN

## ORIGIN

Saffron Gin is based on a recipe that was once lost but then rediscovered, originating from the French colonists in India. Given its new lease of life, the recipe is brewed in the microdistillery belonging to Gabriel Boudier. The recipe is characteristic of colonial times: a gin with exotic botanical ingredients, bursting with flavour and intense aromas. Saffron Gin is made by hand in small batches using saffron. In our opinion, this is a gin you do not come across every day.

## TASTE AND FLAVOUR

Saffron Gin has a deep, orange colour and the aroma of orange and mandarin with subtle notes of the juniper berry. A soft mouth feel and a restrained and slightly delayed saffron taste.

## INGREDIENTS

juniper berry...........................
coriander .................................
lemon.......................................
orange peel..............................
angelica ..................................
orris root.................................
fennel.......................................
saffron .....................................

## COMBINE WITH

don't! Drink neat (with a couple of coffee beans).

# MAVERICKS

There is indeed such a thing as a gin with a temporary character, gins that are created for or during a particular season. We will cover all of them, so allow yourself to be pleasantly surprised by the diversity of gin!

### SLOE (BERRY) GIN
DRINK NEAT OR COMBINE
WITH NEUTRAL TONIC

Sloe gin is a red liqueur which is made by macerating (steeping or infusing) sloe berries in gin, and sometimes also by adding sloe berry juice. The juice can be extracted by adding sugar to the sloe berries. Natural flavourings may also be added to the liqueur. The alcohol content of sloe gin is at least 25 %. Sloe gin is an infusion of fruit with a minimum amount of sugar added. Today, there are several commercial sloe gins which are produced by adding flavourings to cheap, neutral grain alcohol, but there are also producers using the traditional methods, with the recipes for sloe gin varying depending on the distiller. The taste can still be adjusted at the end, but in any case sufficient sugar must be used to ensure the complete extraction of the flavour from the sloe berries. When the sloe gin is properly produced, the alcohol also absorbs an almond-like flavour from the pit of the berry, which gives sloe gin its characteristic taste. Some creators use a shorter steeping time and will instead add almond essence afterwards. Another commonly seen variation adds cinnamon. Sloe gin is perfect on its own, on a cold winter's evening, but it is also excellent when it is mixed in many sorts of cocktail, for example a gin fizz, or try it in wine or champagne. Sloe gin can also give an extra dimension to your gin & tonic.

Sloe (berry) gin can thus either be consumed neat or with a neutral tonic. And to add just a touch of distinction you can also include a little of the original gin from the same makers.

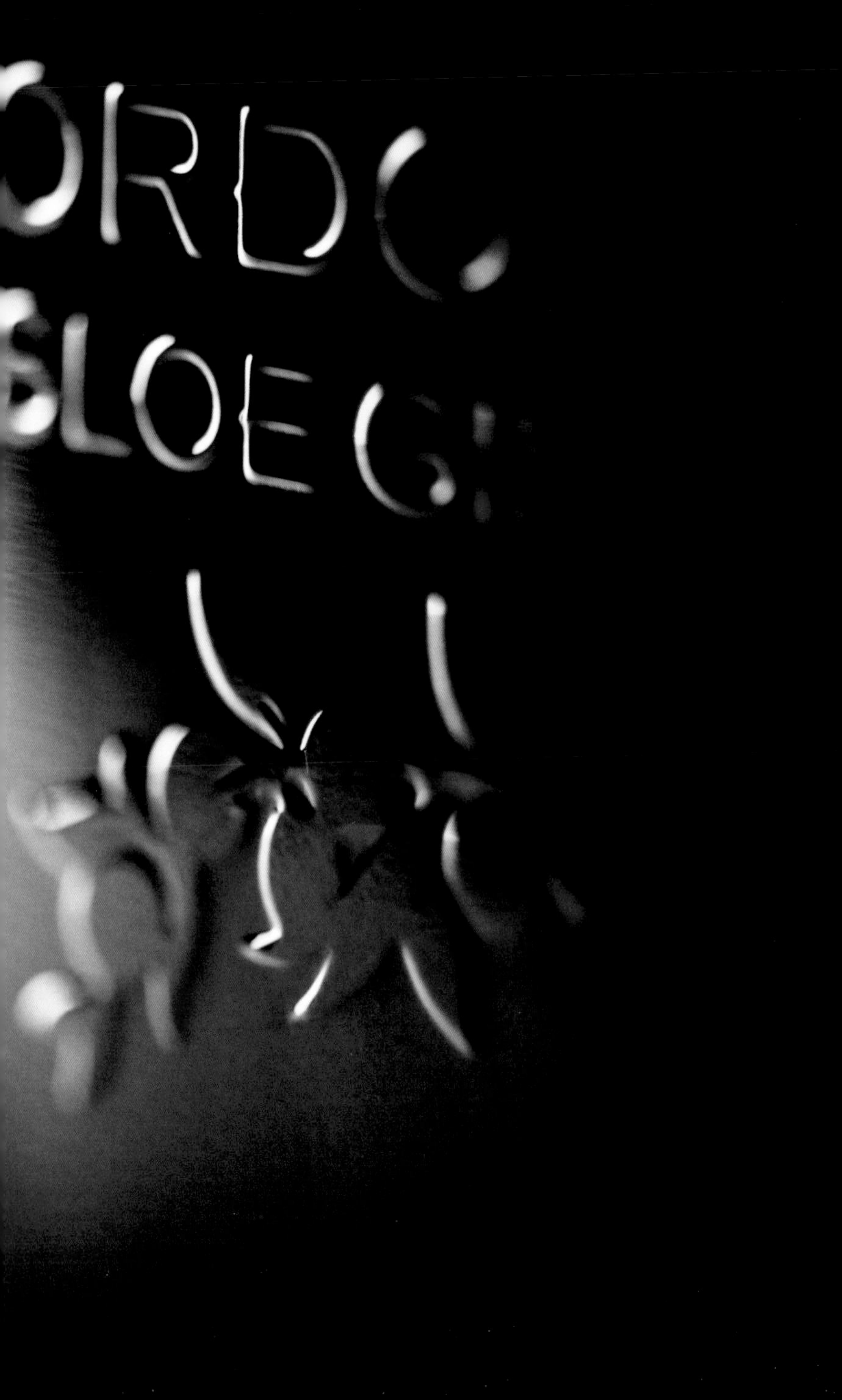

# GORDON'S SLOE GIN

**26 %**

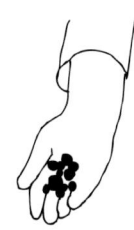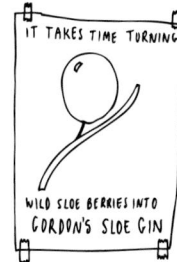

IT TAKES TIME TURNING

WILD SLOE BERRIES INTO **GORDON'S SLOE GIN**

Gordon's Sloe Gin is made with ripe, hand-picked sloe berries, which are brought into balance with a select amount of herbs and spices. Gordon's Sloe Gin has a deep red colour.

## TASTE AND FLAVOUR

The nose of this gin is floral, with a hint of juniper berry and herbs. The taste is well-balanced, with an even-handed fruitiness and an intriguing tone of Earl Grey tea.

## COMBINE WITH

drink neat or with neutral tonic

# MONKEY 47 SLOE GIN

Monkey 47 Sloe Gin is a traditional winter gin, distilled by Christoph Keller for Alexander Stein of the Black Forest Distillers.

**COMBINE WITH**

drink neat or with neutral tonic

THE BLACK FOREST DISTILLERS

## TASTE AND FLAVOUR

Very fresh and fruity, with touches of juniper and almonds. A very high-level sloe gin. The gin is distilled in small batches with 47 botanicals, with the addition of hand-picked wild sloe berries from the Black Forest.

# CAUTION
## WILD ANIMAL

# 26 %

# PLYMOUTH SLOE GIN

Plymouth Sloe Gin is a quintessentially English liqueur based on a recipe from 1883. This gin is the result of using Plymouth Gin which manages to get the most out of the sloe berry extract. The majority of the sloe berries used grow wild on Dartmoor, not far from Plymouth.

## TASTE AND FLAVOUR

Plymouth Sloe Gin has a rich red colour, a result of steeping the sloe berries in strong Plymouth Gin and soft Dartmoor water. The end product is a smooth liqueur taste with a good balance between sweet and bitter fruit flavours, complemented by a hint of almond from the pit of the fruit.

## COMBINE WITH

drink neat or with neutral tonic

# SIPSMITH SLOE GIN

WINTER GIN

**COMBINE WITH**
drink neat or with neutral tonic

The Sloe Gin from Sipsmith is made using frozen, freshly-picked sloe berries to macerate in the gin. The result is beyond compare: silky smooth, blackcurrant, ripe winter fruit and naturally the dominant sloe berry. Sipsmith Sloe Gin is only available in winter months.

## TASTE AND FLAVOUR

The nose offers berries with winter fruit and almonds. On the palate, a strong flavour of blackcurrant with subtle hints of cherry. A velvety finish of balanced sweetness from the berries and sugars complete this cosy gin.

# SIPSMITH®

*independent spirits*

LIMITED EDITION SERIES

*Sloe Gin 2011*

Hand crafted by master distiller:

50cl℮     29%vol

## FRUIT/SUMMER CUP
COMBINE WITH NEUTRAL TONIC
OR A GOOD QUALITY LEMONADE SUCH
AS FEVER-TREE LEMONADE

A fruit cup or summer cup is a traditional English drink, specially created to be mixed as a long drink with a soft drink or mixer. Most fruit cups are developed on a gin base, but there are also vodka-based fruit cups available. As this book is about gin & tonic we will stick to the gin-based varieties here. The gin base is flavoured with various herbs, spices, fruit and botanicals. Fruit cups or summer cups are most popular in the summer months as the name suggests. Manufacturers recommend garnishing the fruit cup with a variety of fruits, vegetables and herbs such as: apple, orange, strawberry, lemon, lime, cucumber, mint, borage and so on. You can certainly allow your creativity to run wild.

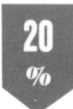

# CHASE SUMMER FRUIT CUP

Chase Summer Fruit Cup is based on Chase Vodka. The distillers begin by warming the vodka in the gin still in order to allow it to pass through the vaporization chamber and mix with 17 botanicals. The distillate is then combined with naturally purified water from the aquifer (an underground water bearing rock layer) which runs underneath the distillery's apple orchard. Following this, a carefully selected blend of elderflower, locally grown raspberries and blackcurrants are added to the gin in varying ratios.

## TASTE AND FLAVOUR

Earl Grey tea, rosemary and thyme in the nose, which is followed by the floral aromas of raspberry, elderflower and lavender. In the mouth, ripe and juicy blackcurrant and raspberry. In the background, tones of star anise and ginger. To finish, the fruit cup surprises you with the flavours of rosemary and thyme again, rounded off with lemon.

## COMBINE WITH

neutral tonic or a good quality lemonade

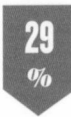

# SIPSMITH SUMMER CUP

**29 %**

EARL GREY TEA

**COMBINE WITH**

neutral tonic or good quality lemonade

This fruit cup is based on Sipsmith London Dry which is blended with an array of carefully selected summer ingredients, including an infusion of Earl Grey tea, lemon verbena and cucumber. Aromatic but surprisingly dry, this fruit cup lends itself well to the addition of fruit and lemonade.

## TASTE AND FLAVOUR

The nose is reminiscent of fresh oranges and fresh cucumber, underpinned by the delicate tones of tea. The juniper berry and the citrus are clearly present in a taste which is enriched with herbs and hints of cherry. The finish is complex but still refreshing.

## SEASONAL GIN

A seasonal gin is literally named: a limited edition gin launched for a particular summer or winter season.

The flavours are so diverse so that each case has to be assessed individually when it comes to combining with tonic.

# BEEFEATER®

## LONDON DRY GIN

## LONDON MARKET

### *Limited Edition*

A VIBRANT GIN WITH
POMEGRANATE, CARDAMOM
& KAFFIR LIME LEAF

POMEGRANATE

KAFFIR LIME

#  40 % BEEFEATER
## LONDON MARKET
## LIMITED EDITION

BEEFEATERS · DESMOND PAYNE ·

**COMBINE WITH**
neutral tonic

This limited edition was brought out in 2011 and developed by Beefeater's master distiller, Desmond Payne. London Market Gin is based on the original Beefeater Gin but enjoys the addition of extra botanicals such as pomegranate, kaffir lime leaves and cardamom.

### TASTE AND FLAVOUR

The aroma of redcurrants, vanilla and lime greets your nose. The classic juniper berry, citrus and subtle spices are also clearly present. The taste of the lime and orange peels are complemented by the juniper and bitter orange. The pomegranate is much more subtle in the mouth than on the nose, while the cardamom and the well-thought-out spicing adds to the flavour. The finish is citrusy with tones of bitter herbs, liquorice and peppery spices.

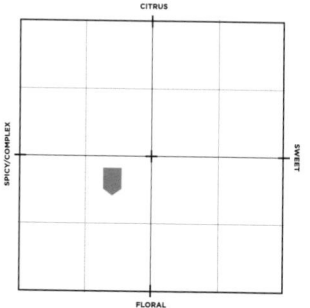

# FILLIERS TANGERINE
## SEASONAL EDITION

For the summer of 2013, master distiller Pedro Saez Del Burgo created this special seasonal edition with one unusual ingredient (which also happens to be Pedro's favourite fruit), the tangerine. Pedro chose quality tangerines from Valencia in Spain, which are harvested between November and January. During the cold Belgian winter months, the tangerines are brought to the fifth generation Filliers distillery. Filliers Tangerine Seasonal Edition is available from May until the 2013 stock sells out.

## TASTE AND FLAVOUR

Filliers Tangerine Seasonal Edition is a perfect base to use in cocktails or long drinks. It has a soft, fruity taste with clear accents of fresh orange and tangerine, interwoven with a mixture of herbs. The juniper berry is clearly present, filled out with cardamom giving a full, warm flavour. Notes of coriander and pepper make the gin surprisingly spicy, while the Belgian hops contribute a hint of bitterness. This Filliers Tangerine Seasonal Edition brings Spanish temperament to your glass, offering the mood of a sultry summer evening.

## COMBINE WITH

aromatic tonic

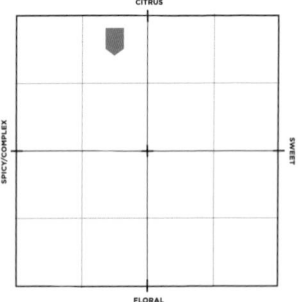

SMALL BATCH · HANDCRAFTED

# Filliers Gin 28

TANGERINE · SEASONAL EDITION

## NAVY STRENGTH GIN
COMBINE WITH NEUTRAL TONIC,
BUT EASY ON THE GIN!

Navy Strength gin is a gin which is bottled with an alcohol percentage of 57%. Navy Strength gin grew from the idea of 'proof spirits' (literally meaning proved spirits). The term proof spirits began in the 18th century when rum was dished out to British soldiers. To be sure of the quality of the rum, gunpowder was added and then the mixture was ignited. If it didn't catch fire, it meant that the rum contained too much water and was therefore marked as being 'under proof'.

Navy Strength gins have a higher alcohol percentage than the original versions and therefore prove their value in mixing present-day cocktails. So be careful with the amount of gin that goes into your 'strong' gin & tonic.

# hernö

navy strength

...ANIC SWEDISH NAVY STRENG...

3

48|21H

...OL 50 L ORGANIC SWEDISH GIN CRAFTED BY HERNÖ...

# HERNÖ
# NAVY STRENGTH

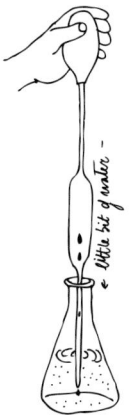

Hernö Navy Strength is manufactured in the same way as Hernö Swedish Excellence Gin. The only difference is in the water content. While the original Hernö is diluted to a 40.5% alcohol percentage, the navy strength version is diluted to 57%. The difference in taste and feel is very noticeable: the character of the botanicals come more strongly to the fore due to the high alcohol content.

## TASTE AND FLAVOUR

Perfectly balanced with the aromas of fennel, coriander, dry pine, beeswax and citrus. There are also some lighter flowery notes.

**COMBINE WITH**
neutral tonic

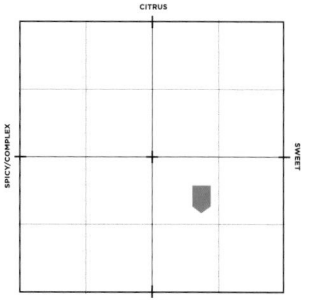

# 57 %

# PLYMOUTH
## NAVY STRENGTH

For almost two centuries, the Royal Navy has never left port without a bottle of Plymouth Navy Strength on board. Plymouth Navy Strength Gin is made in the same way as the classic Plymouth Gin, with the same combination of botanicals distilled in a copper, pot still and a neutral grain alcohol. The only difference is that Navy Strength is bottled with an alcohol content of 57%.

### TASTE AND FLAVOUR

For some, Plymouth Navy Strength is the ultimate gin with a rich yet wonderfully balanced taste, which can elevate a Martini or gin & tonic to a higher level. Perfect for the demands of today's more adventurous drinkers and mixologists. The high alcohol content strengthens the flavours and aromas of the herbs, but maintains the supple and balanced character for which Plymouth Gin is so famous.

**COMBINE WITH**
neutral tonic

*Other available brands offering a Navy Strength version are: Pimlico (United Kingdom), Leopolds Navy (United States), FEW Standard Issue (United States), Hayman's Royal Dock (United Kingdom), Perry's Tot (United States) and Bathtub Gin Navy Strength (United Kingdom).*

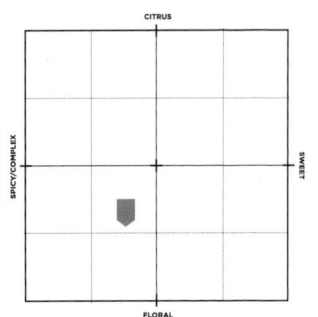

## DISTILLER'S CUT
COMBINE WITH NEUTRAL TONIC
OR DRINK NEAT

A Distiller's Cut gin is a unique version of the standard gin; whereby the master distiller creates a 'no holds barred' variety.

Due to the intense flavour sensations, we recommend drinking it neat. If however, you do want to mix these gins we suggest choosing a neutral tonic.

# BLACK GIN
## DISTILLER'S CUT

Black Gin Distiller's Cut has, just like its brothers, no less than 74 botanicals from 19 different countries, and is produced by the Gansloser Distillery. This version is extra spicy thanks to the increased alcohol content.

### TASTE AND FLAVOUR

The contents are not to be outdone by the design of this mysterious bottle. A combination of aromas immediately greets the nose. On the palate a whole host of ingredients play with each other. The finish is spicy, sometimes referred to as medicinal.

### COMBINE WITH

drink neat or with neutral tonic

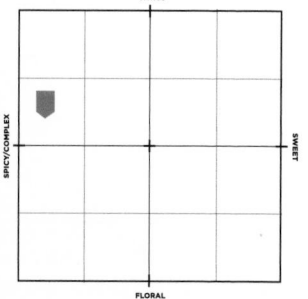

# MONKEY 47
# DISTILLER'S CUT

**COMBINE WITH**

drink neat or with
neutral tonic

This special limited edition from Monkey 47 gin is a more complex and fuller-flavoured variety than the standard version. The Distiller's Cut has been left to mature for longer in earthenware vats which allow the flavours to become more refined. This version of Monkey 47 is the personal creation of master distiller Christoph Keller. It is a complex gin, distilled three times and not cool filtered. There are only 2,500 bottles of this gin produced per year.

## TASTE AND FLAVOUR

An appealing and complex nose with the typical characteristics of a London Dry: juniper berry and peppery notes. In the nose as well as in the mouth, the Distiller's Cut is crisp, fresh and fruity. The lengthy maturing process ensures a good balance of all the components. An extremely complex and full-bodied gin.

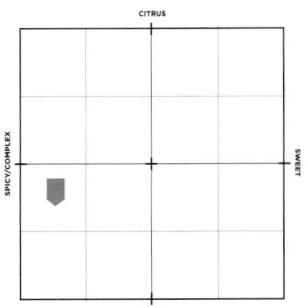

# SPRING GIN GENTLEMAN'S CUT

Longer on top

slight fade to the top

Short around the ears

GENTLEMAN'S CUT

The Gentleman's Cut is the jewel in the crown of Spring Gin and contains the same ingredients as the classic version, but with an extra punch. Spring Gin was launched by Manuel Wouters, owner of the SIPS cocktail bar in Antwerp.

## TASTE AND FLAVOUR

This gin is extremely clean-tasting, guaranteeing the freshness of the citrus flavours. A richer mouth feel than the original version. Very delicate in taste with hints of aniseed and coriander.

**COMBINE WITH**

drink neat or with neutral tonic

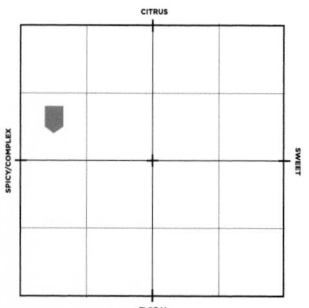

CITRUS

SPICY/COMPLEX

SWEET

FLORAL

The

ORIGINAL

· BRAND ·

# SPRING GIN

DRINKS NEVER TASTE THIN WITH SPRING GIN

A Handcrafted Limited Run of 900 Bottles of which this is

No. 725

DISTILLED IN FLANDERS

48.8% Vol (97.6 Proof), ℮ 500ML

Gentleman's Cut

### PINK GIN
COMBINE WITH
NEUTRAL TONIC

Pink gin is based on the cocktail popular in 19th century Britain when a few drops of angostura bitters were added to gin. Angostura bitters is a drink which was first made in 1824 by Dr J. Siegert as a remedy to reduce the symptoms of fatigue and stomach complaints. Angostura is made from more than forty tropical herbs and plant extracts and has a spicy taste. The name derives from the harbour town Ciudad Bolívar in Venezuela, which used to be called Angostura.

RTON

*Pink*

GIN

& BOTTLED

# EDGERTON PINK GIN

## COMBINE WITH

neutral tonic

Edgerton Pink Gin has pomegranate to thank for its seductive blush, and is London's first Pink gin. This super-premium gin is distilled in London and sources its ingredients from all over the world: juniper berries, coriander, angelica, orris root, sweet orange peel, cassia bark and nutmeg are all left to infuse together for 24 hours.

### TASTE AND FLAVOUR

The first thing you notice is the scent of the sweet pomegranate which is added after distillation. The sweetness disappears almost immediately as you take your first sip and is replaced by an explosion of warmth. Sour and not too complex. Maybe one for the ladies?

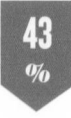

# LEBENSSTERN PINK GIN

BERLIN

Lebensstern Pink Gin is a premium gin specially developed for the Bar Lebensstern in Berlin. The gin is flavoured with the fresh aromatic bitters from 'The Bitter Truth'.

## TASTE AND FLAVOUR

Lebensstern Pink Gin has a rich, spicy taste, with just a touch of sweetness. Complex and intense.

**COMBINE WITH**

neutral tonic

# LEBENSSTERN
### Bar im Einstein

# PINK GIN

Development GmbH
Reutlingen, Germany
ES.com
Contains certified color E 129

e700 ml

43 % vol.

9

# THE BITTER TRUTH
## PINK GIN

---

The Bitter Truth Pink Gin is a delicious mix of traditionally crafted gin and aromatic bitters. Designed to suit modern tastes, it enjoys a soft and friendly mouth feel alongside delicate, complex flavours.

### TASTE AND FLAVOUR

The nose of this fragrant gin is dominated by complex fruity and flowery aromas. The taste is very supple with the distinctive flavours of juniper in the foreground, surrounded by the spicy aromas of liquorice, caraway and fennel.

**COMBINE WITH**
neutral tonic

# RANSOM

*Alambic Pot Distillation*

*Heart Cuts*

*Barrel Aged for 3 to 6 Months*

Ingredients: malted two row barley, corn, juniper berries, or
peel, lemon peel, coriander seed, cardamon pods, & angelica

**Handcrafted from Naturally Farmed Grains and Botani**

Batch No: 032    Bottle No: 0494

Alcohol 44% by Volume (88 Proof), 750mL

## AGED GIN
DRINK NEAT

It may come as a surprise, but there are indeed a few aged gins. Some are left to rest for a short period while others are matured for years in wooden vats. The colours are as varied and stimulating as the tastes. Here we pick out three.

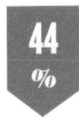

# CITADELLE
## RÉSERVE GIN

### ORIGIN

Citadelle Gin, as cited before, is a French gin from the Cognac region which uses 19 different types of herbs and spices, and is distilled three times. The original Citadelle Gin is officially a London Dry, but makes a few adjustments in the production process. Unusually small boilers are used, heated by a 'naked' flame, signifying that no steam is released during the process. The Reserve is made in batches of only 21 barrels and then matured for two years in Limousin oak vats.

### TASTE AND FLAVOUR

The fragrance is light and elegant and very appealing. Mild notes of juniper berry and lemon followed by the woodiness from the Limousin oak vats. Lightly sweet in taste with the trio of juniper berry, oak and citrus. Followed by a mild but solid spiciness which is complemented by a light earthiness.

### INGREDIENTS

juniper berry from France .....
Moroccan coriander ...............
orange peel from Mexico .......
cardamom from India .............
liquorice from China ...............
cubeb pepper from Java .........
French flavourings ..................
Mediterranean fennel .............
Italian orris root ......................
cinnamon from Sri Lanka ......
French violets ..........................
almonds from Spain ...............
cassia from Indochina ............
German angelica ......................
grains of paradise from West Africa .....................
Dutch cumin .............................
nutmeg from India .................
Spanish lemons .......................
star anise from France ...........

### COMBINE WITH

don't, drink neat!

# COLOMBIAN AGED GIN

**43%**

## ORIGIN

This gin comes from the makers of Dictator Rum and is left to mature for six months in the Dictator Rum vats. The gin is distilled five times.

## TASTE AND FLAVOUR

Golden in colour and full-flavoured with woody tones, vanilla, spices and dried fruit.

## INGREDIENTS

juniper berry............................
berries ......................................
spices ......................................
botanicals.................................
tropical citrus peel.................
and others

## COMBINE WITH

don't, drink neat!

COLOMBIA

*Aged Gin*

AGED IN RUM BARRELS BY
DICTADOR

Old Tom
Gin

# RANSOM

*Alambic Pot Distillation*

*Heart Cut!*

*Barrel Aged for 3 to 6 Months*

Ingredients: malted two row barley, corn, juniper berries, orange peel, lemon peel, coriander seed, cardamon pods, & angelica root.

**Handcrafted from Naturally Farmed Grains and Botanicals**

Batch No: 032    Bottle No: 0494

Alcohol 44% by Volume (88 Proof), 750mL

# RANSOM OLD TOM

**44 %**

## ORIGIN

Ransom Old Tom Gin is manufactured by the Ransom Wine Company in Oregon (USA). The pharmacy-style bottle invokes the Wild West and cowboys and Indians. This Old Tom Gin is a blend of two distillations which are then combined to give one batch. This batch is then distilled again. One distillate consists of a malted grain mash (similar to whisky) and the other is a neutral grain distillate to which herbs are added. The blend is then allowed to lay in cleaned Oregon Pinot Noir vats for six months. This maturing process gives the gin its beautiful straw colour, making it soft and full of character. Ransom Old Tom Gin is absolutely one of a kind.

*Batch No: 001*
*Bottle No: 0001*

## TASTE AND FLAVOUR

In the nose, a soft whisky or a dynamic gin. The subtle mouth feel is a result of the use of a malted barley base, combined with an infusion of corn alcohol. You taste, amongst others, mint, pimento berries, cardamom and a light hint of juniper berry.

## INGREDIENTS

juniper berry.............................
orange.........................................
lemon..........................................
coriander ..................................
cardamom.................................
angelica .....................................

## COMBINE WITH

don't, drink neat!

### DAMSON GIN
COMBINE WITH NEUTRAL
TONIC OR DRINK NEAT

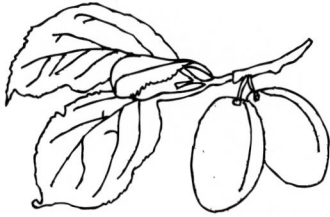

Damson gin is actually a liqueur which bears a strong similarity to sloe gin, in both the idea and how it is produced. In this case a few whole Damson fruits are allowed to macerate for at least eight weeks in sugar, to form a syrup. Damson gin is popular particularly in Great Britain, and is often just made at home and drunk around Christmas.

# OUR 14 MOST REMARKABLE GINS

The history of gin has already spanned several centuries, but it is perhaps in the last few years that the evolution has been at its most frenzied. That is why we have chosen our 14 most remarkable gins to demonstrate our interpretation and views of this revolution. Without prejudice towards other brands, we have a deep respect for these particular manufacturers and everything they have achieved over the past months, years and centuries in the world of this highly remarkable sprit. You as the reader may not agree with our selection, or perhaps you will revel in it or just be surprised. Or maybe you will decide on the ultimate tribute and seek out these 14 selected gins, to try or to add to your collection. It's all up to you! Here are also our suggestions for the complete gin & tonic.

# ORIGIN GIN

## THE BASIC ONE

A basic gin could not be more basic: only differentiated by the juniper berry and local waters. To understand gin in its purest form, it is perhaps necessary that we take a moment to go a little deeper into the basic ingredient, the juniper berry. Basic but oh so important. The juniper berry is not only the key ingredient, and the most important botanical, but its presence is actually a legal requirement. The aroma and taste of the juniper berry should at the very least be the signature of every gin, both in the nose as well as in the mouth. Even the name of gin itself is derived from the juniper berry. Therefore, allow us a moment to pay homage to the juniper berry, as without it, gin would not even exist.

The juniper is a small evergreen tree or bush which can grow to a height of nine metres. It takes about two years before the berries are properly matured. There are around sixty or so different species and they grow in the majority of countries in the northern hemisphere. They can even be found growing at a height of 3,500 metres. If the juniper berry was a grape, winemakers would certainly be jumping for joy. As we all know, the soil, the climate and the growing conditions all have an impact on grapes. The term 'terroir' is used to denominate vineyards, and is moreover the first feature of a good wine. Following this logic, the provenance of the juniper is also significant when it comes to judging a gin.

It is interesting to know that the juniper tree is dioecious, meaning there are both male and female plants. An individual plant can only produce male or female berries, and you will never find both male and female berries on the same tree.

We can safely say that the uses for juniper vary widely: from bath oil to flavourings, and from spice to natural medicine for all sorts of ailments. The Egyptians, the Romans, the Greeks... all used juniper for something. The wood of the tree was also utilized although not as widely as the berries, mostly for its smoke and the aroma that is given off when the wood is burned.

The aroma of the juniper berry itself also has a big impact on our perception of the taste and varies from region to region, bringing us back to our terroir...

So there are — just as with wine, coffee and chocolate — origins of single estate gin distillates available, each with their own taste and character. We will describe four of these below, but due to the unsurpassed popularity of gin there are already several single origins available and it is highly likely that even more are being made at this very moment.

**46 %**

ITALY
# ORIGIN AREZZO
# LONDON DRY GIN

This Italian juniper features a clean nose of soft pine needles. Creamy and with a hint of citrus. When other botanicals are added to the distillate, together they form a beautifully rounded gin: warm with a mildly spicy conclusion.

**COMBINE WITH**
Fever-Tree Tonic Water and juniper berry

**46 %**

THE NETHERLANDS
# ORIGIN MEPPEL
# LONDON DRY GIN

The juniper from the Netherlands has an almost woody, earthy taste. Hints of tobacco and a slightly longer finish than the Italian juniper. Creamy, but complemented by a note of sweetness. The finish is more complex than the Italian distillate.

**COMBINE WITH**
Fever-Tree Tonic Water and juniper berry

**46 %**

ALBANIA
# ORIGIN VALBONE
# LONDON DRY GIN

The juniper from Albania is a special case and clearly demonstrates how the origins of the berry can determine the taste. Red fruits, cocoa, dry. When other botanicals are added, the distillate maintains its character but then with a lively sweetness.

**COMBINE WITH**
Fever-Tree Tonic Water and juniper berry

**46 %**

BULGARIA
# ORIGIN VELIKI PRESLAV
# LONDON DRY GIN

The distinctive flavour of the juniper dominates even when other botanicals are added. The sharp perception of alcohol both in the nose and in the mouth is featured.

**COMBINE WITH**
Fever-Tree Tonic Water and juniper berry

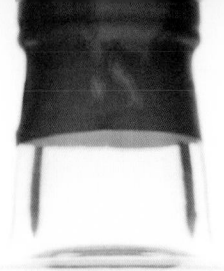

### WASHINGTON ISLAND
#### WISCONSIN

EST.

# DEATH'S DOOR

2005

MADE WITH ORGANIC HARD RED WINTER
WHEAT FROM WASHINGTON ISLAND, WI.
SIMPLE ◇ LOCAL ◇ EXCEPTIONAL

*Crafted with wild juniper berries*
& VARIOUS ORGANIC BOTANICALS

### ••• GIN •••

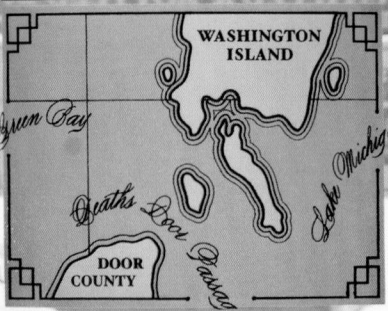

WASHINGTON
ISLAND

Green Bay

Lake Michigan

Deaths Door Passage

DOOR
COUNTY

70CL • 47% ALC. BY VOL.

UNITED STATES

**47,3 %**

# DEATH'S DOOR GIN

## THE SIMPLE ONE

### ORIGIN

Washington Island in Wisconsin is the beating heart of Death's Door Gin. The name is inspired by the notorious water way Death's Door between Washington Island and the Door County Peninsula. Death's Door Spirits work with local farmers whose produce is of exceptionally good quality. The distillery was founded in 2005 by Brian Ellison, and this gin is a perfect example of beautiful simplicity. It is remarkable that Death's Door Gin can draw out so much flavour from just three botanicals: juniper berry, coriander and fennel seed. The juniper berries are picked on the island with the other ingredients carefully selected from the state of Wisconsin. The grain alcohol used is wheat-based and is also grown on the island: after more than 35 years with no agriculture on the island, brothers Tom and Ken Koyen began cultivating wheat again in 2005. A good decision, in our opinion.

### TASTE AND FLAVOUR

Death's Door Gin is characterised by the spicy taste and aroma. The juniper berry takes the upper hand, but at the same time is complemented by a warm and peppery deepness.

### INGREDIENTS

juniper berry............................
coriander .................................
fennel seed ..............................

### COMBINE WITH

Abbondio Tonica Vintage Edition and a marshmallow

BRIAN ELLISON

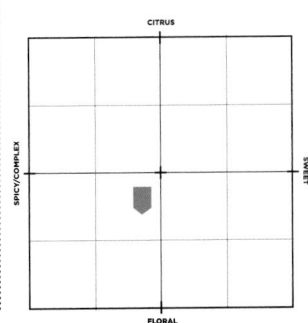

# 52,3 % NOLET'S RESERVE

## THE EXPENSIVE ONE

### ORIGIN

With a yearly production of only a few hundred bottles, an extremely careful selection procedure and the application of four generations of production knowhow via Carolus Nolet Senior, this Nolet's Reserve is one of the most exclusive, rarest and most expensive gins ever made. The Nolet distillery is still brewing in Schiedam, and still in its original location. The gin has a recommended retail price of 650 euro, so there really is only one way to enjoy this gin: sip slowly, to comprehend its full complexity. An exclusivity to be proud of, and to give the whole experience a touch more flair, each bottle is numbered and signed by Mr Nolet himself.

### TASTE AND FLAVOUR

Strawberries and flowers in the nose. Warm and complex on the palate where a whole host of flavours are slowly revealed: saffron, peach, raspberry, citrus and, of course, juniper berry. A warm and lightly spicy glow of saffron (the most expensive spice) and subtle delicate lemon verbena feature in this gin.

### INGREDIENTS

juniper berry............................
saffron ...................................
lemon verbena........................
and other botanicals

### COMBINE WITH

don't, drink neat!

- 1 0 0 BOTTLES MAX -

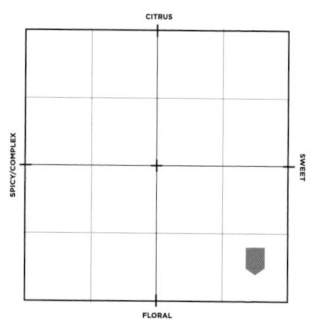

# NOLET'S
## DRY GIN

### THE RESERVE

IMPORTED

# BOMBAY SAPPHIRE

## THE REVOLUTIONARY ONE

### ORIGIN

Bombay is a light London Dry Gin which was brought out from under the dust covers of London gin in the late 80s — 1987 to be precise. Now distributed by Bacardi, the recipe has been used by the Bombay Spirits Company since 1761 and makes use of ten different botanicals. Revolutionary to its very core and maybe one of the reasons for today's craze for gin, with its fashionable looks and image giving a boost to the dowdy perception of gin. The character of Bombay Sapphire is a perfect way to attract vodka drinkers, and to entice them into the world of gin. The juniper berry is less dominant in this aromatic gin compared with other more classic styles. Bombay is set apart by the distillation methods used in the Carter head still. The herbs and spices are not distilled directly in the still itself, but are instead placed in a basket in the neck of the boiler. This allows for the flavours to be gently absorbed by the alcohol vapours. It is thanks to this method, which creates the delicate and light palate that is so appreciated by vodka drinkers. This gin is still popular in night clubs, and will certainly remain so.

### TASTE AND FLAVOUR

An aroma of juniper berry and citrus, but also pepper and spices are clearly present. On the palate, this gin tastes delicate, lightly fruity with the different herbs and spices slowly coming through when holding the gin longer in your mouth. The finish is short.

### INGREDIENTS

Italian juniper berry...............
orris root....................................
Spanish almonds.....................
Spanish limes...........................
grains of paradise from
West Africa................................
Moroccan coriander...............
Chinese liquorice....................
cassia bark ...............................
angelica from Saxony..............
tailed pepper from Java..........

### COMBINE WITH

Fever-Tree Tonic Water and lime zest and flaked almonds

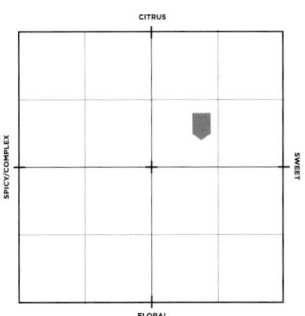

# VL92 GIN

## THE RETRO ONE

41,7 %

-VL92-

## ORIGIN

VL92 Gin was borne out of a quest of two
entrepreneurs, Leo Fontijne and Sietze
Kalkwijk, who went in search of the ultimate
gin. This Dutch artisan gin uses malt
wine (25%) in its production, the original
ingredient of jenever, and is therefore strongly
reminiscent of the origins of jenever and gin.
The gin is named after an historic Dutch
sailing ship which was used for transporting
exotic spices, too daring for the local jenever
recipes of the time, but perfect for VL92 Gin.
On 15th May 2012, the first batch of VL92 Gin
was delivered to London, arriving in style on
the original ship.

## TASTE AND FLAVOUR

The malt wine is responsible for the boldness,
the complexity is delivered by the play of the
botanicals, and the surprise is brought about
by the coriander leaf. The inspired addition of
malt wine cannot be found in any other gin.

## INGREDIENTS

malt wine ....................................
juniper berry .............................
coriander leaf ...........................
and various other botanicals

## COMBINE WITH

Fentimans Tonic Water
and a sliver of ginger

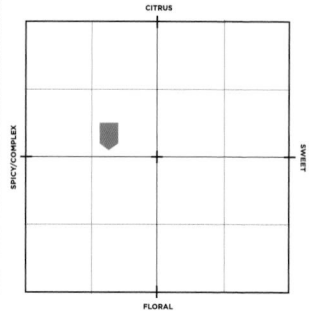

CITRUS

SPICY/COMPLEX

SWEET

FLORAL

# VL92 GIN

ginstooksel:

| | | | |
|---|---|---|---|
| moutwijn | | | XX |
| korianderblad | /// | | XY |
| | | | |
| 28 JUL 2013 | | | YY |
| | | | |

41.7% alcohol per volume
1000ml.

H. van Toor Jz.
Distilleerderij
VLAARDINGEN HOLLAND

**44,5 %**

# ZUIDAM
# DUTCH COURAGE

## THE HISTORICAL ONE

SHOT

### ORIGIN

Zuidam Distillers is one of the last remaining independent distilleries in the Netherlands, and the family-run business makes its own distillate and extracts using traditional methods of working and production. The name of the gin is a historical reference to the shot of jenever given to the soldiers in the thirty years' war, before they were sent into battle. Zuidam Dutch Courage Dry Gin has been awarded many times at big international competitions.

### TASTE AND FLAVOUR

On the nose, strong and spicy aromas with a core of earthy juniper, filled out with exotic herbs. The taste is earthy with a hint of citrus and dried herbs. A bittersweet and intense finish.

### INGREDIENTS

juniper berry..............................
coriander ...................................
angelica .....................................
oranges and lemons
from Spain .................................
Madagascan vanilla ................
Indian liquorice.......................
cardamom pods
from Ceylon .............................

### COMBINE WITH

Thomas Henry Tonic Water and a liquorice stick

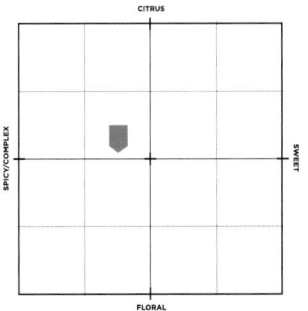

# 43,3 % BATHTUB GIN

## THE MYTHICAL ONE

### ORIGIN

An unusual gin created by the enigmatic Professor Cornelius Ampleforth. Shortly before he gained the title of Professor, Cornelius, a mad inventor, dreamed of running a big laboratory full of botanical spirits, bubbling beakers and miles of glass bottles filled with rare ingredients. His dreams came true at the end of 2011, with the release of his already infamous Bathtub Gin. The name is a nod to the gin that people enjoyed during prohibition in the 1920s. Bathtub Gin is only produced in very small quantities of thirty to sixty bottles each time. The brown paper packaging of the gin catapults the drinker back in time to the Victorian chemists.

### TASTE AND FLAVOUR

Initially a full bouquet of juniper in the nose, which is complemented by rich grain alcohol. Notes of cardamom and orange blossom and a hint of cinnamon fill out the flavour. The focus of the taste is the juniper berry, but the earthy botanic spices stimulate the palate. The mouth feel is syrupy and, towards the finish, the juniper makes way for the cardamom and cinnamon.

### INGREDIENTS

juniper berry............................
orange peel................................
coriander ..................................
cinnamon...................................
cardamom..................................
cloves........................................

### COMBINE WITH

Schweppes Premium Mixer Original Tonic and a cinnamon stick

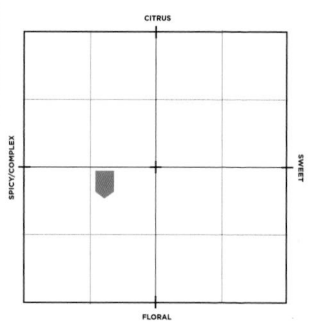

# Professor Cornelius Ampleforth's

# athtub G

# BLACK GIN

## THE COMPLEX ONE

### ORIGIN

Black Gin is produced at the Gansloser Distillery and is the most complex of gins on the market, with no less than 74 botanicals from 19 different countries such as Germany, Italy, Spain, India, Madagascar and Romania. Of the 74 botanicals, 68 are distilled in a macerate which is inky black in colour, hence the name. An absolutely unique gin with a limited issue.

### INGREDIENTS

juniper berry...........................
lemon peel ...............................
orange peel ..............................
ginger.......................................
coriander .................................
bay ..........................................
and 68 other botanic ingredients we can only guess at

### COMBINE WITH

Original Premium Tonic Water Classic and zest of lime

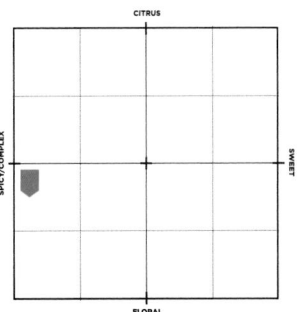

# HOXTON GIN

**43 %**

## THE EXTREME ONE

BARTENDER SALVATORE CALABRESE

## ORIGIN

Developed by the son of the famous barman Salvatore Calabrese in Hoxton — the creative centre of London — it can be described as unique for its kind. The gin is made using alcohol obtained from French summer wheat and a medley of natural ingredients. The botanicals are steeped for five days before they are distilled in 150-year-old copper pot stills. After completion, Hoxton Gin rests for two months in steel tanks. A truly surprising gin with the taste of coconut and grapefruit. Amongst purists there is much discussion as to whether it can even be classed as a gin at all. Taste it and decide for yourself.

## TASTE AND FLAVOUR

Coconut and grapefruit predominate in the nose, although the ginger, juniper berry and tarragon are also discernible in the background. The taste is also dominated by the coconut and grapefruit. Here, the juniper plays second fiddle.

## INGREDIENTS

juniper berry............................
coconut.....................................
grapefruit..................................
orris root..................................
tarragon....................................
ginger.......................................

## COMBINE WITH

J. Gasco Indian Tonic and a piece of coconut

# HOXTON GIN

# WARNING!
## GRAPEFRUIT
### AND
#### COCONUT

# -ish

## LONDON DRY GIN

*Irresistible Scandalous Hallmar*

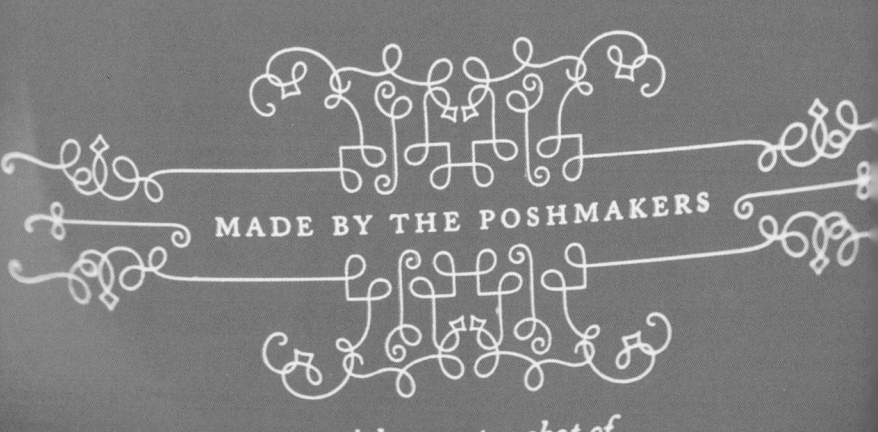

MADE BY THE POSHMAKERS

*with an extra shot of*
*Juniper*

# ISH GIN

## THE DRY ONE

**I**RRESISTIBLE

**S**CANDALOUS

**H**ALLMARK

41 %

---

### ORIGIN

Irresistible Scandalous Hallmark is represented by the initials ISH in this premium gin. Ish Gin is a traditional London Dry style gin, but with a little something extra: a double shot of juniper which makes it the driest of London Dry gins. Ish Gin was thought up by Ellen Baker and is Spanish-inspired, via her 'Bristol Bar' in Madrid. A perfectly balanced recipe that provides a distinctive flavour profile without the use of artificial additives. Ish Gin is distilled five times in a traditional pot still, in the heart of London.

### TASTE AND FLAVOUR

A definite juniper berry aroma with coriander and refreshing citrus. On tasting this gin, the orange is immediately noticeable, followed by a harmony of other botanicals.

### INGREDIENTS

juniper berry ...........................
coriander seed ........................
angelica .....................................
almonds.....................................
orris root ...................................
nutmeg ......................................
cinnamon ..................................
cassia..........................................
liquorice ....................................
lemon peel ................................
orange peel ...............................

### COMBINE WITH

1724 Tonic Water and dried juniper berries

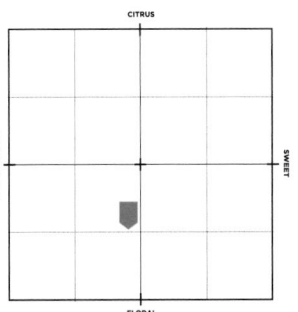

# TANQUERAY MALACCA

## THE PHOENIX ONE

### ORIGIN

Tanqueray Malacca was for years seen as the little brother of the widely known Tanqueray London Dry Gin. Founded in 1997 — based on a recipe from 1839 — the gin was taken off the market in 2001, despite its growing popularity amongst gin lovers. Following this, record amounts were paid on the black market by people wanting to get their hands on a bottle of this iconic gin. In 2013, the label was relaunched to the general public. The reintroduction issue of this spicy gin consists of a mere 100,000 bottles worldwide. An homage to the recipe from 1839, taken from the notes of Charles Tanqueray, the gin was developed during his trade missions to the Far East, with herbs and spices from all four corners of the world. Nowadays, trying to locate a bottle is like looking for a needle in a haystack. But definitely worth the effort!

### TASTE AND FLAVOUR

Tanqueray Malacca is a lighter and fruitier gin, with less juniper but more grapefruit aroma than its big brother. The gin is soft and round with a prominent cinnamon, almost candy-like taste. The finish is simple and clean.

### INGREDIENTS

No information available

### COMBINE WITH

Gents Swiss Roots Premium Tonic and grapefruit zest

CHARLES TANQUERAY

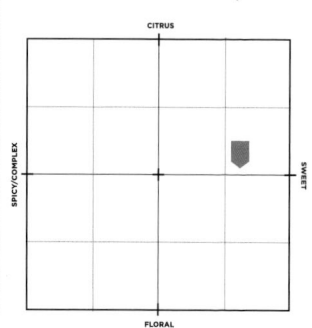

# Tanqueray
## MALACCA GIN
### LIMITED EDITION

IAN OCEAN

BOTTLE Nº: GR 0638

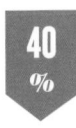

# SACRED GIN

## THE VACUUM ONE

### ORIGIN

Sacred Gin is one of the standard bearers of microdistilleries, a sub-trend of the gin revival. Creators Ian and Hillary Hart produce the gin in their own terraced house in North London, where they have an artisan distillery. Sacred Gin is Ian's brainchild, brought to life in 2008 after he lost his job as a head-hunter. He dusted off his degree in natural sciences and started to concentrate on vacuum distillation. He tried out his gin on friends at the local pub and, on the 23rd attempt, it was unanimously declared a success. Sacred Gin is produced under a very low pressure, but this does not compromise the quality; quite the contrary. Each of the twelve organic botanicals are macerated in the finest quality English grain alcohol, and then separately distilled in glassware under high pressure. This process ensures the fresh and luxuriant character, and is above all highly unusual in the world of gin. The name 'Sacred' comes from one of the botanicals: Olibanum or 'Boswelia Sacra' in Latin (a type of incense).

### TASTE AND FLAVOUR

Spicy in the nose with citrus notes. Soft tastes of nutmeg and juniper berry, leading to an elegant finish.

### INGREDIENTS

juniper berry............................
freshly cut lemon ....................
cardamom.................................
nutmeg .....................................
incense Boswelia Sacra...........
and others

### COMBINE WITH

Fever Tree Indian Tonic Water, grated nutmeg and/or cinnamon stick

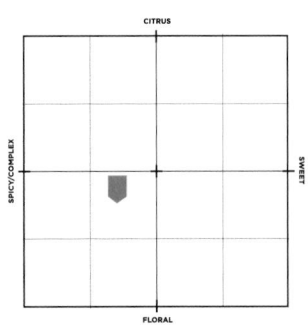

# 7 DIALS GIN

## THE COMMUNITIES ONE

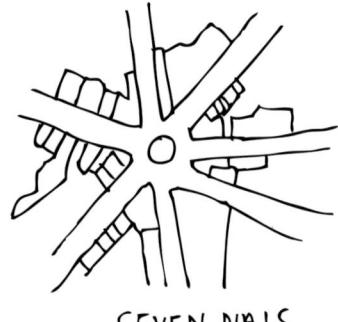

SEVEN DIALS

## ORIGIN

This London Dry Gin is named after the famous crossroads in the St. Giles district of London. Seven Dials is between St. Giles and Soho. In the late 1600s, seven streets were laid, converging at this point to make a star. During the 1700s, this area was the base for tens of gin shops. 7 Dials Gin is produced by the London Gin Club and makes use of seven botanicals.

## TASTE AND FLAVOUR

On the nose, a fresh pine and light floral hint. The taste begins with spice and a strong dose of cardamom, expanded with juniper berry and coriander.

### INGREDIENTS

juniper berry.............................
coriander ..................................
angelica ....................................
marshmallow root ..................
clementine peel.......................
cardamom.................................
almonds....................................

### COMBINE WITH

Schweppes Premium Mixer Original Tonic and zest of lemon and lime

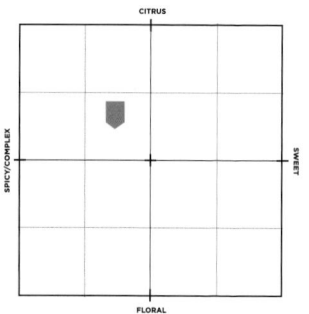

# 7 Dials

## LONDON DRY GIN

GIN, HAPPY PRODUCT OF OUR CITY, CAN SINEWY STRENGTH IMPART, AND WEARIED WITH FATIGUE AND TOIL, CAN CHEER EACH MANLY HEART. LABOUR AND ART UPHELD BY THEE, WE SUCCESSFULLY ADVANCE. WITH CHEER, GENIUS LIQUID, THY PINTY TASTE ENLIVENS EVERY DANCE. IMPS, AND WARMS EACH ENGLISH BREAST WITH LIBERTY AND LIFE.

# HENDRICK'S GIN

## THE MARKETING ONE

### ORIGIN

Hendrick's Gin is popular, very popular. They call themselves the Monty Python of gins: full of humour and fun. Hendrick's is a super-premium gin with an unusual twist. Hendrick's is distilled in Ayrshire, Scotland, which boasts centuries of distilling expertise, as well as soft Scottish water from the local Penwhapple Burn. Hendrick's Gin is made using eleven botanical ingredients, including Belgian and Dutch cucumbers and Bulgarian rose. The cucumber and rose petal flavours are in fact added afterwards as an infusion. The new apothecary-style bottle and the innovative way of serving with cucumber was ground-breaking and gave the entire gin sector a serious boost when it was launched in 2000. The gin is made in two different distillation vessels: one a Carter-Head and the other a copper Bennet still. This delivers two different spirits which are then blended together: one, a soft citrus spirit, the other, full of character, making Hendrick's a crisp gin with a flowery aroma. Hendrick's is crafted using traditional methods through which the distillation process can be carefully fine-tuned. In 2003, *The Wall Street Journal* named it the best gin in the world.

### TASTE AND FLAVOUR

A refreshing gin with a strong character, subtle flavours and a delightful aroma. This is due, amongst other things, to the essence of Dutch cucumbers and the oils of Bulgarian rose petals.

### INGREDIENTS

juniper berry...........................
chamomile................................
caraway seeds.........................
elderflower..............................
meadowsweet.........................
orange peel..............................
coriander ................................
orris root.................................
angelica ..................................
lemon peel..............................
cubeb berries.........................

### COMBINE WITH

Fentimans Tonic Water and cucumber

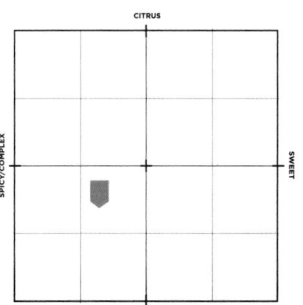

# THE PRACTICAL: IN THE MIX

## PURE PASSION

Gin, and of course tonic, have now become so incorporated in the world that it is high time that we put the theory into practice, and show you how it should be done: the right proportions, tools and garnishes.

Put on some laid back music, grab a gin & tonic and move to the beats of this ideal partnership. The pure love which has manifested for decades; passion since the first meeting, a moment of rest and then a rekindled 'love at second sight'. And believe us, this renewed passion is one that makes the sparks fly, one that invites delirious dancing or can, just as in the game of love, sometimes maintain a kind of 'coolness'. A love where both partners challenge each other, enhance and lift each other up and encourage creativity. But stay open-minded as there is a third player in this relationship — Mr or is it Mrs Botanical? (We will leave this choice to your own imagination) — may often accompany the couple and can even improve them; a couple with just that little bit extra, which you will notice in your glass...

## HOW IT SHOULDN'T BE...

Let us give you a couple of silly examples: a bowl of cornflakes with champagne or a bag of chips with caviar. To say the least, these are strange combinations, but also combinations that have virtually no common ground with very few similarities as far as taste interest or creativity go. Although it must be said, each product individually has its own qualities, but they just don't work when put together. Some things are just not meant to be. Just like chips and caviar do not provide the basis for a long-term relationship, some gins do not blend well with certain tonics.

# HOW TO FIND THE PERFECT MIX AND USE THE G&T FLAVOUR CROSS

First of all, you need to find out who you are in terms of which gin you enjoy the most. Happiness lies in your own hands, as they say, and happily the search for your personal favourite gin is a lot of fun. To begin with, taste as many as you can, which of course can be done at the same time as enjoying the summer on a terrace, going dancing and investigating the range on offer at the disco, or relaxing by the open fire at home. Of course take this book with you and discover, read and record. However, don't forget that every journey of discovery has its ups and downs, sometimes a gin will sound lovely when you read about it, but disappoint when you taste it, or the other way round. Look at it as a quest that may last throughout your whole life, and may well change direction, but one thing we can promise you: your own Holy Grail exists! After that, it becomes even more fun and maybe even easier, because this book will steer you in the right direction, give you lots of inspiration to find the right tonic and show you how to make and serve the ultimate gin & tonic.

As you now know, the secret behind the perfect mix is actually quite simple. It is all about analysing the ingredients in both the gin and the tonic. On the following pages, we will introduce an original way of examining flavours: the G&T flavour cross.

# G&T
# FLAVOUR CROSS

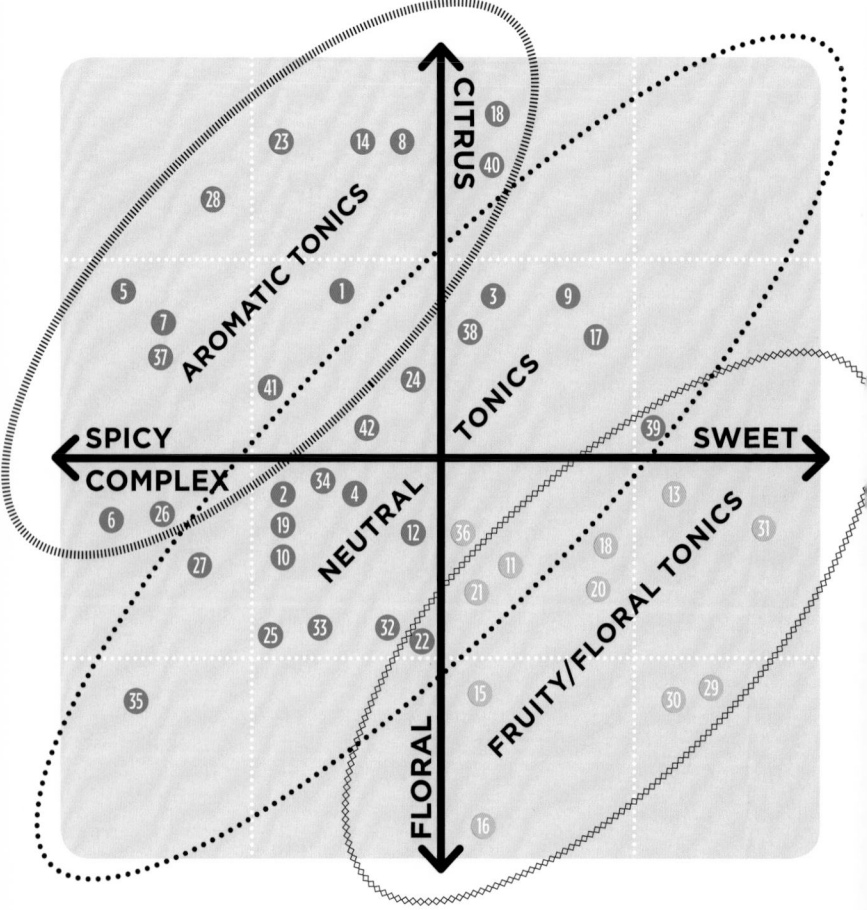

## GINS

1 — 7 Dials Gin
2 — Bathtub Gin
3 — Beefeater Gin
4 — Beefeater London Market
   Limited Edition
5 — Black Gin Distiller's Cut
6 — Black Gin
7 — Blue Gin
8 — Bluecoat
9 — Bombay Sapphire
10 — Bulldog Gin
11 — Citadelle Gin
12 — Death's Door Gin
13 — Fifty Pounds
14 — Filliers Tangerine
   Seasonal Edition
15 — G'Vine Floraison
16 — Geranium Gin
17 — Greenall's London
   Dry Gin Export Strength
18 — Haswell Gin
19 — Hendrick's Gin
20 — Hernö Navy Strength
21 — Hernö Swedish
   Excellence Gin
22 — Ish Gin
23 — London Nº3
24 — Martin Millers Westbourne
   Strength Dry Gin
25 — Mombasa Club Gin
26 — Monkey 47 Distiller's Cut
27 — Monkey 47
28 — Nº209
29 — Nolet's Reserve
30 — Nolet's Dry Gin
31 — Old English Gin
32 — Plymouth Gin
33 — Plymouth Navy Strength Gin
34 — Sacred Gin
35 — Saffron Gin

36 — Sipsmith Gin
37 — Spring Gin Gentleman's Cut
38 — Tanqueray Export Strength
39 — Tanqueray Malacca
40 — Tanqueray Rangpur Gin
41 — VL92 Gin
42 — Zuidam Dutch Courage

## NEUTRAL TONICS ·················

— 6 O'Clock Indian Tonic Water
— Abbondio Tonica Vintage Edition
— Aqua Monaco Tonic
— Britvic Indian Tonic
— Fever-Tree Indian Tonic
— J.Gasco Indian Tonic
— Original Premium Tonic
— Seagram's Premium Tonic
— Schweppes Premium Tonic
— Thomas Henry Tonic

## AROMATIC TONICS ||||||||||||||||||||||||||||||

— Fentimans Tonic Water
— Fever-Tree Mediterranean Tonic
— Original Premium
   Tonic Water Blue

## FRUITY/FLORAL TONICS ∞∞∞∞∞∞∞∞

— 1724 Tonic
— Indi Botanical Tonic
— Gents Swiss Roots
   Premium Tonic
— Original Premium Tonic Pink
— Q Tonic
— Schweppes Premium Tonic
   Pink Pepper
— Schweppes Premium Tonic
   Orange Blossom & Lavender
— Thomas Henry
   Elderflower Tonic

Have you already taken a good look at the G&T flavour cross? This innovative new version shows the combination of the flavours of gin and of tonic, it is an absolute first and very easy to read and interpret.

### LET'S PRACTICE!

First, take your favourite gin of the moment or go and get the bottle you were given as a present, but if you are not sure which tonic to combine it with, it's OK, we will wait for you....

Have you got it? Right, now get the G&T flavour cross with the gin universe and the tonic tastes. Open the bottle, smell the aroma, taste the pure gin. But hang on, we haven't explained how to correctly taste gin yet...

### TASTING THE GIN

Although humans can distinguish between many different tastes, there are actually only four different kinds of taste papillae, each specialised in detecting a specific taste: sweet, salty, sour and bitter. All the flavours we can distinguish are combinations of these four basic tastes. Now, there is also a fifth taste, 'umami' or savoury that can be added to the list. Although this was scientifically recognised in 1980 as one of the basic tastes, it is only since 2010 that people have started to refer to umami as the fifth taste.

The five basic tastes however, are only a part of how we perceive tastes. For humans, the sense of smell plays an important role in taste. A smell can give a certain expectation of what you are about to taste. So it is going to be interesting to see if the gin lives up to those expectations or not.

And so, to work...

SWEET

SOUR

SALTY

BITTER

UMAMI

**THE GLASS**

SNIFTER   ALSO GOOD   TUMBLER (NO GOOD)

The glass can help with the tasting. It is preferable to use a tulip-shaped glass with a wide base but narrower at the rim as this will better help the aromas channel towards the nose. This type of glass is called a snifter, but a similarly shaped wine or sherry glass will do just as well. A tumbler (a broad glass with a thick bottom and straight sides) is not so good for tasting as the aromas dissipate quickly.

**THE GIN**

Pour about 30 ml of gin into the glass. You can also add a little water as this dampens down the alcohol and enhances the taste of the botanicals used.

**ROLL**

Roll the gin around the glass. This adds oxygen and allows the aromas to gather on the edge of the glass. By doing this it will allow you to perceive the bouquet of the gin more effectively.

### THE NOSE

Put your nose into the glass — literally — and sniff in the fragrance. A few common terms used to identify the aromas in gin are: citrus, fruity, floral, earthy, spicy, sweet and woody.

*Note:*
A strong chemical odour is an indication that you are dealing with a poor-quality gin.

### THE TASTE

Take a little sip and swirl the gin around in your mouth to evaluate the elementary tastes. Then let the gin rest on the tongue before rolling it around in your mouth again, allowing you to analyse all the flavours.

The first sip should feel warm and pleasant with the subtle flavour of juniper berries. Take the time to give all the flavours a chance to come through, because as you already know, there is a whole range of botanicals used in the development of a gin.

Following this, try to find the dry taste of the gin. A dry feeling on the back of your tongue often means that there have been a lot of herbal botanicals used, such as angelica or orris root.

Many commonly-used terms to describe the tastes of gin are first and foremost the four 'arms' in our flavour cross: citrus, sweet, floral, and spicy/complex. But tastes are also often described as earthy, peppery, exotic and so on.

### THE FINISH

Finally, a feature of a good gin is that it should always leave a fresh and clean finish. The juniper berry flavour shouldn't hang around for too long. When you are ready to take your next sip, the previous one should only be a memory, gins with this quality are often said to be soft.

### GIVING THE GIN A PLACE ON THE FLAVOUR CROSS, AND FINDING THE RIGHT TONIC

We have already placed a lot of gins on the flavour cross, but if you have discovered a good gin of your own, after tasting you will want to give your discovery its own place on the flavour cross. Focus mainly on the citrus, sweet, floral and herby/complex tastes. The closer your gin is to the centre of the cross, the closer it is to the classic London Dry taste. If you find it impossible to place your gin anywhere on the flavour cross, it is more than likely an exotic gin. These types of gin need to be individually assessed when it comes to the choice of tonic.

**A QUICK RECAP:**

### CLASSIC LONDON DRY

London Dry gins find themselves in the central part of the flavour cross and so should not be coupled with a strongly pronounced tonic. They are better partnered with a more neutral tonic such as Fever-Tree Indian Tonic Water, Thomas Henry Tonic Water or a Schweppes Premium Mixer Original Tonic. A neutral tonic will perfectly enhance the classic flavours of a London Dry without overpowering it.

### CITRUS GIN

These gins are inordinately suited to aromatic tonics, and an aromatic tonic with a citrus note is absolutely ideal. For example, combine with Fentimans Tonic Water infused with lime leaves, amongst other things. These ingredients perfectly highlight the citrus notes in your gin.

### SWEET GIN

The average sweetness of these types of gin are best combined with the flavours of a fruity tonic, such as 1724 Tonic Water and Indi Botanical Water.

### FLORAL GIN

The typical characteristics and botanicals used in these types of gin, with the light fruitiness and beautiful floral bouquets, are very much at home with the soft and fruity composition of tonics such as 1724 Tonic Water and Indi Tonic Botanical Water.

### SPICY GIN

Spicy gins clearly display a pronounced palette of aromas and flavours, and because of this complex diversity, they blend perfectly with an aromatic tonic such as Fentimans Tonic Water. But one could also argue that because these types of gin are so complex and multi-layered, they only need the slightest lift. This is certainly understandable: the spiciest of gins like Monkey 47 of Gansloser Black Gin — are so great already, a neutral tonic *is all they need.*

### DON'T FORGET TO EXPERIMENT!

We are focusing on 100% natural tonics, but you should absolutely explore for yourself the vast range of gins and the countless brands of tonic that are available. For example, think about the gins which use elderflower as an ingredient, such as Darnley's Gin, Knockeen Gin, Zephyr Gin, etc. These gins go very well with Thomas Henry Elderflower Tonic.

The sky is the limit, and your own creativity and experience will certainly bring about knowledge. Experimentation is free, and don't forget that there are new brands of gin and tonic emerging almost every week, providing enough material for endless mixing and matching, and discovering surprising new combinations.

Once you have found your perfect pair (or sublime mix), we can proceed with the ideal way of serving this melodious couple. We begin with the classic way of serving and the correct proportions. Don't worry, we will discuss 'the perfect' serve shortly, including of course the garnish.

# THE CLASSIC GIN & TONIC

Let's begin with the basics: a gin & tonic, nothing more and nothing less. The recipe is simple, but still deserves the appropriate attention. Something simple can so easily be diminished by not taking the time or paying too little attention. So pay attention and you will never forget it. Sloppiness is no excuse in the world of cocktails, where even the basics are an art form. The classic measurements used are: 1 measure of gin to 4 measures of tonic. The tonic must complement the essence and purity of the gin and not dominate.

— 1 measure gin: 50 ml
— 4 measures tonic: 200 ml tonic
— A lot of ice

1 X GIN          4 X TONIC          ICE (A LOT)

The bigger the ice cubes, the better, as water is actually the enemy of gin & tonic so you need to do everything possible to make sure the ice melts as little as possible.

And lemon or lime, we hear you say... Well really that depends on the natural flavours of the gin. This distinguishes it from, for example vodka. Without a doubt the juniper berry is the protagonist, but very often this taste is supported by lemon or lime. In other words, the citrus taste is already present. If however, you wish to enhance this flavour or add a little more citrus to a gin where this flavour is not strong enough, then by all means you should do so. *De gustibus et coloribus non disputandum est* — in matters of taste, there can be no disputes. Our advice? When you do decide to add lemon or lime to a gin & tonic, just add the peel or zest of the fruit, otherwise the juice and the acid will overpower the 'real' taste of the gin.

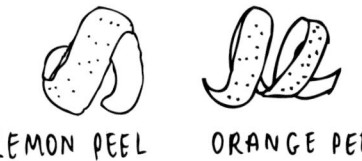

LEMON PEEL          ORANGE PEEL

**Note:**
*The purists and connoisseurs amongst us will doubtless prefer a slightly stronger gin & tonic. In that case the ratio can easily be adjusted to 1 measure of gin to 2 or 3 measures of tonic, or even 1 measure of tonic. But to get the optimal enjoyment out of the phenomenon that is gin & tonic, the 1 to 1 proportion is the minimum requirement.*

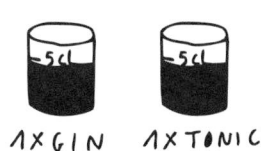

1X GIN     1X TONIC

# THE PERFECT SERVE

Just as a meal should look appealing to stimulate the appetite, a gin & tonic should be just as tempting and invite you to quench your thirst. Spain is the birthplace of contemporary gastronomy (it is no coincidence that they have dominated the international restaurant guide lists), and so the Spanish have also elevated the gin & tonic to an art form. Moreover, 'gintonic' is a way of life in Spain, it is omnipresent, a 'ginsanity' that is impossible to ignore. About five years ago, it was the interest of Spanish chefs, and above all the bartenders, who gave the drink a serious boost, and it became incorporated into Spanish culture. Now, locals and tourists alike can enjoy the ritual that is all part of the perfect serve...

## THE GLASS

Gin & tonic is served in a large 'copa de balon' or balloon glass: similar to a large wine glass that, as the name suggests, is balloon-shaped. A tumbler, a short, broad cylindrically-shaped glass is also ideal for serving a gin & tonic. If you use a long drink glass, you trap the gin at the bottom. A copa glass or tumbler gives a wider surface area for the gin & tonic which the mix can only benefit from. A broad glass will also help release the aromas, of which some will be captured in the glass due to the slight narrowing at the top. You see: every detail counts...

### THE ICE

Large ice cubes made from 'clean water' that hasn't come into contact with other products. Ice will quickly take on the smells and flavours of other products kept in the same freezer. The larger the ice cube, the less chance it will melt, and as mentioned earlier, you don't want your gin & tonic diluted down by water. Here it is a case of the more, the better. By all means fill your glass to the brim with ice cubes, a gin & tonic should be cold!

BIG ICE
CUBES

*Note:*
*You can of course cool the glass by first rolling ice cubes around in the glass. Make sure you replace the ice cubes with fresh ones after cooling.*
*A creative spirit? Try freezing a botanical in the ice cube itself. Not only does it look pretty, but it also won't have much effect on the taste of your gin & tonic.*

### THE GIN

There is no such thing as the best gin in the world. Everyone has their own personal taste. 5 cl (50 ml) gin is the standard measure and is easy to judge with a jigger as they mostly hold 5 cl (50 ml). If your personal choice has a higher alcohol percentage (+45%), we recommend that you use a little less gin.

THE JIGGER

## THE TONIC

The starting point is 1 measure of gin to 4 measures of tonic. This means 50 ml of gin with 200 ml tonic is the ideal partnership. Not all bottles of tonic contain 200 ml, however. Fentimans for example, only has 125 ml, while Q Tonic comes in a bottle of 237 ml. You should always ask that your gin and tonic is served separately so that you can pour your own drink, and your friends can then enjoy any leftover tonic. Too little tonic? Well, then you can drink your gin & tonic with a bit more zing. Do you drink gin & tonic mostly at home? In which case there is no problem, as you are the bartender and after reading this book you will know exactly how to serve your perfect gin & tonic. Pour the tonic against the side of the glass: this will keep the bubbles at their best, or make use of a bar spoon, allowing the tonic to gently flow over the spoon handle and into the glass.

## GARNISHING A GIN & TONIC, SENSE OR NONSENSE

As we have already discussed, making a salad of your favourite gin & tonic is not the idea. We will leave the discussion about whether to use a garnish or not, for now. You and you alone can decide what finally goes into your gin & tonic. First and foremost, the garnish is for the attractive presentation of the glass, but can also highlight a particular taste or provide an additional taste that is missing. The principle is straightforward:

How do you choose the right garnish? Above all, keep it simple. Research which ingredients and botanicals are included in the makeup of your gin, this can either be by using this book, searching the internet or sometimes on the bottle itself. Make a choice: either you want to enhance a partic-

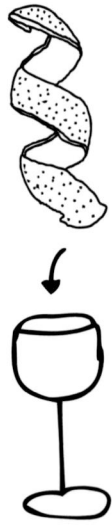

ular taste already in the gin or you want to add a subtle flavour accent.

When you have decided to add a garnish to your gin & tonic, don't forget this simple, but oh so important rule: always wash fruit, herbs or anything else you may use. Another important point: when using citrus fruit as a garnish (lemon, lime, orange) only use the peel or zest, as this is the part that contains the oil of the fruit without the bitterness of the pith.

### UTENSILS AND CUTTING TECHNIQUES

A traditional zester is used to cut very fine strips from the peel of a citrus fruit. With a fine peeler it is also easy to cut slightly larger citrus zest strips. Of course a good knife is indispensable. If you decide to add spices to your gin & tonic, don't go overboard: a twist of the pepper mill, 1 star anise, 3 juniper berries, 1 or 2 grates of nutmeg, etc., should be sufficient. Whichever cutting techniques and creations you choose is of course completely up to you. Your own creativity and humour will certainly lead to new discoveries and ways of garnishing. Nevertheless, we do want to take a close look at one of the most commonly used methods of cutting citrus peel, namely the twist. Peel the skin of a citrus fruit with a fine vegetable peeler, take an end of the strip in each hand and twist the zest strip in opposite directions above the glass to release the oils. Finally, let the twist sink into the glass.

Just as in the general tone of our book, the emphasis should be on combining the right gin with the right tonic. The garnish is just the final touch, and should be a gentle touch at that, and not too fussy.

Easy does it, always...

### THE FINISH

Stir your creation briefly with a (bar) spoon or swizzle stick, two or three stirs should be plenty. But our most important tip for the perfect finish: drink it in good company...

# GINLICIOUS: FOOD & GIN & TONIC

People who are of the opinion that gin & tonic is destined to stand all alone have got it wrong. Many dishes, from tapas to desserts, find an ideal companion in gin & tonic. Gin & tonic not only sharpens the palate, but also offers a totally new taste sensation. Gin is definitely a bottle full of possibilities: a gin & tonic can either perfectly complement the flavours in your meal, or can act as an ingredient in the recipe, or both. Gin has inspired many a gastronome to create surprising combinations, and it is no longer possible to imagine the culinary world without it.

Pull up a chair and get ready for this 'ginlicious' experience. The chefs serving up this feast are Hermes Vanliefde and his side-kick Peter Laloo, managers of the unique Rock-Fort in Bruges. They really know how to get the most out of the bottle, and create magic both on the plate and in the glass standing next to it...

"To form the perfect link between the dish and the gin & tonic, we serve them 'clean', without garnish."

Each recipe is for four people.

## GIN-TONIC:
# HENDRICK'S GIN + FENTIMANS TONIC WATER

## RECIPE:
# TUNA TARTARE, GRANITA OF APPLE AND ROSE WATER, WITH CUCUMBER

The cucumber taste that is so redolent in Hendrick's Gin is mirrored in this dish. The freshness of the granita offers a delightful contrast, and simultaneously forms the perfect link to the gin & tonic.

### PREPARATION

Combine all the ingredients for the sauce, mix and pass through a sieve. Finely chop the tuna and mix with 2 to 3 tablespoons of the sauce. Season to taste with pepper and salt. Next, add the chopped shallot, chives and sesame seeds. Combine thoroughly.

Mix all the ingredients for the granita together in a shallow freezer-proof container. Place in the freezer but check after an hour or so and loosen with a fork as the ice crystals form.

Soak the dried seaweed in lukewarm water. Allow to drain thoroughly and combine with a little of the sauce. Garnish the tuna with the seaweed, cucumber and apple slices. Finish with the Hendrick's granita.

### INGREDIENTS

200 g tuna
(from the Mediterranean) ..............
salt and pepper .......................
1 large French shallot, chopped ...................................
2 tsp. chopped fresh chives....
20 g dried seaweed .................
½ cucumber, finely diced ......
1 Granny Smith apple, in slices...................................
1 tbsp. sesame seeds................

### Sauce
30 g grated fresh ginger..........
60 ml sushi-vinegar ................
100 ml Arbequina olive oil.....
30 ml soy sauce.......................
a little sesame oil.....................

### Granita
200 ml apple juice ..................
40 ml Hendrick's Gin..............
100 ml white wine ..................
1 tsp. rose water.......................
3 tbsp. cane sugar syrup .........

# GIN-TONIC:
## GERANIUM GIN + 1724 TONIC WATER

# RECIPE:
## FRESH GOAT'S CHEESE WITH JUNIPER BERRY, PRESERVED LEMON AND HONEY

Goat's cheese and juniper is a wonderful combination, and the connection to the gin goes without saying. The preserved lemons perfectly complement the floral and slightly herby notes in the Geranium Gin, which contains, amongst other ingredients, the oil of the geranium plant. The dish is finished off with a garnish of geranium petals.

**PREPARATION**

Pre-heat the oven to 180 °C.

Cut eight lengthways slices of the courgette on a mandolin, and then cut the slices into thin ribbons. Season with salt and pepper.

Season the goat's cheese with the juniper berries, pepper and salt, spoon the honey over the cheese and grill until soft, or brown with a blow torch.

Arrange the courgette-spaghetti on the plates, place the goat's cheese on top and finish with a slice of preserved lemon and the geranium petals.

**INGREDIENTS**

1 courgette ...............................
4 goat's cheese .........................
4 dried juniper berries............
pepper and salt........................
4 slices preserved lemons (available from speciality suppliers or Moroccan stores)........
4 tbsp. honey.............................
20 (approx.) geranium petals .........................................

## GIN-TONIC:
# FIFTY POUNDS GIN + 1724 TONIC WATER

## RECIPE:
# GLASS NOODLES WITH SEAFOOD AND SEAWEED

---

**Fifty Pounds Gin is a sweet gin which combines perfectly, or perhaps contrasts with, the saltiness of the sea flavours of the seafood. The seaweed and samphire also play their part perfectly.**

### PREPARATION

Combine all the ingredients for the vinaigrette and keep in a squeezable dressing bottle.

Steep the dried seaweed in lukewarm water and allow to drain well. Then mix with the vinaigrette.

Cook the cockles and mussels for a short time, in a pan or on a plancha covered by a lid.

Briefly cook the glass noodles and allow them to cool under cold-running water. Then mix with the seaweed and vinaigrette. Remove the oysters and mussels from their shells, but leave the cockles whole, and arrange all the ingredients on a plate.

### INGREDIENTS

100 g dried seaweed ...............
20 cockles ..................................
20 Bouchot-mussels ...............
150 g glass noodles...................
100 g samphire ........................
4 Oysters (Gillardeau)................
12 fresh coriander sprigs........

*Vinaigrette*
2 tbsp. grated fresh ginger .....
2 tbsp. sushi-vinegar ..............
2 tbsp. soy sauce ......................
9 tbsp. Arbequina olive oil .....
a little sesame oil.....................

# G'VINE FLORAISON +
# FEVER-TREE INDIAN TONIC WATER

## VERJUICE MARINATED FOIE GRAS, MUSCAT GRAPES, RAISINS, JAMON IBÉRICO, BREAD CRUNCH AND FENNEL

The basis of G'Vine Floraison Gin is the Ugni Blanc grape. The verjuice (the juice of unripened grapes) used in this dish perfectly complements the gin. The fattiness of the foie gras is counterbalanced by the acidity of the verjuice. The flavours of grapes (and raisins) are also echoed in the dish.

**PREPARATION**

For the bread crunch: in the peanut oil, fry the bread cubes with the garlic and rosemary. Allow to drain for two days, then blitz into fine crumbs.

Cut the raw foie gras into slices. Marinate for 15 minutes in the verjuice, season with salt and pepper, the raisins and grapes.

Arrange the foie gras on a plate, garnish with the Jamon Ibérico, a tablespoon of the bread crunch, a few sprigs of fennel leaf and dress with a little of the juice from the grapes and raisins.

**INGREDIENTS**

100 g foie gras ...........................
200 ml verjuice (juice of unripened grapes) .........................
pepper and salt .........................
24 dark raisins .........................
12 Muscat grapes, quartered ...................................
4 slices Jamon Ibérico ...........
a few fresh fennel leaf sprigs ...................................

*Bread crunch*
1 small stale white loaf, roughly cut into cubes ...........
1 clove garlic .............................
1 sprig fresh rosemary .............
1 litre peanut oil .......................

# GIN-TONIC:
## GIN MARE +
## 1724 TONIC WATER

# RECIPE:
## HAND-PEELED ZEEBRUGGE PRAWNS, CHERRY TOMATOES, ARBEQUINA OLIVES AND BASIL

---

The bouquet of Gin Mare is reminiscent of a bunch of ripe tomatoes. The cherry tomatoes in this recipe are therefore the perfect partner, forming a bridge between the prawns and the gin. The botanicals in Gin Mare include, amongst others, rosemary, thyme, Arbequina olives and basil. The rosemary and thyme flavours are present in the vinaigrette, and the dish is finished with basil and olives, which matches the gin and tonic seamlessly.

**PREPARATION**

First make the vinaigrette. Warm the white wine vinegar slightly to about 50 °C, along with the tomato, shallot and fresh herbs. Allow to infuse for 15 minutes off the heat and then pass through a sieve. Add the olive oil.

Blanch the cherry tomatoes in boiling water, then plunge into a bowl of iced water. Peel before adding to the vinaigrette.

Arrange the tomatoes on the plate and garnish with the olives, prawns and basil leaves.

**INGREDIENTS**

20 cherry tomatoes.................
16 Arbequina olives ................
100 g cooked hand-peeled .....
Zeebrugge prawns...................
12 sprigs fresh small
leaf basil .....................................

*Vinaigrette*
50 ml white wine vinegar ......
1 tomato, peeled
and chopped.............................
1 shallot, finely chopped.........
fresh thyme
(according to taste) ........................
fresh rosemary
(according to taste) ........................
fresh oregano
(according to taste) ........................
60 ml Arbequina olive oil.......

## GIN-TONIC:
# BLUE GIN +
# FENTIMANS TONIC WATER

## RECIPE:
# WILD DUCK WITH BEETROOT, POMEGRANATE, CLOVES AND BLACK PEPPER

The spicy finish of Blue Gin, with its surprisingly earthy tone, combines beautifully with the wild duck, cloves and black pepper. The gin is also used in this recipe's preparation.

**PREPARATION**

Pre-heat the oven to 180 °C. Cook the duck filet with plenty of black pepper and the cloves, then finish by baking in the oven for about 12 minutes. Add the pomegranate vinegar and the Blue Gin to the pan. Remove the duck filets and keep warm.

Finish the sauce off in the pan with the brown stock and a knob of butter.

Cook the beetroots in water with salt and vinegar. Once cooked through, remove the skins and then reheat in a pan with some butter, sugar and pomegranate vinegar.

Arrange the sliced duck and beetroot on the plates, finish with the sauce, a few pomegranate seeds and sprigs of fresh mint. Season with a final grind of fresh black pepper.

**INGREDIENTS**

2 wild duck filets......................
black pepper (freshly ground)....
2 cloves.....................................
2 x 1 tbsp. pomegranate vinegar.................................
60 ml Blue Gin..........................
500 ml beef stock....................
a knob of butter.......................
8 small beetroots.....................
a pinch of salt...........................
2 tbsp. distilled white vinegar............................
3 tbsp. brown sugar ................
a knob of butter.......................
500 ml water.............................
1 fresh pomegranate ...............
4 sprigs of fresh mint..............

# FILLIERS TANGERINE SEASONAL EDITION + FENTIMANS TONIC WATER

RECIPE:
# CEVICHE OF SEA BASS, CITRUS, TOASTED CORN AND CORIANDER

Tangerines are used in the making of this seasonal edition of Filliers Gin. **Filliers Tangerine Seasonal Edition has a soft, fruity taste, with clear accents of fresh orange and tangerine. The citrus flavours in the gin are reflected by the mix of citrus fruits in the dish, which at the same time combine flawlessly with the ceviche of sea bass.**

## PREPARATION

First prepare the ceviche by dissolving the palm sugar in a little water. Next add the lime zest, lime juice and mandarin or orange juice.

Make the coriander oil by combining the roughly chopped coriander with the grape seed oil and warm to 80 °C before passing through a sieve.

Remove the dark parts of the sea bass and cut into thin slices.

Divide the ceviche into the serving bowls and arrange the slices of sea bass on top. Finish with the coriander oil, red onion, chili peppers and the toasted corn.

## INGREDIENTS

+/- 280 g sea bass filet.............
1 red onion, chopped...............
1 red chili pepper, chopped....
a handful of toasted corn
or crunchy corn chips
(health food store) .........................
4 kumquats (small elongated
orange-like fruit) ...........................

### Coriander oil
1 bunch fresh coriander..........
100 ml grape seed oil...............

### Ceviche
1 tbsp. palm sugar.....................
juice and zest of 1 lime............
juice of 2 mandarins
or 1 orange ................................
3 tbsp. Arbequina olive oil .....

# GIN-TONIC:
## MOMBASA CLUB GIN
## + FENTIMANS TONIC WATER

# RECIPE:
## CRÈME OF WHITE CHOCOLATE, GRAPEFRUIT, GRANITA OF MOMBASA CLUB GIN, STAR ANISE, CANADA DRY AND VERBENA

Gin is also excellent when included in the preparation of a dessert, and here is a good example. Based on Mombasa Club Gin, this spicy granita counterbalances the rich crème of white chocolate. The citrus hints in the gin are enhanced by the grapefruit and the spicy notes are highlighted by the use of star anise and the ginger of the Canada Dry.

### PREPARATION

Mix the egg yolks with the sugar. Warm the milk and cream together, then add to the egg yolk mixture. Continue to heat to 85 °C and then add the soaked gelatine leaves. Sieve the mixture and strain over the white chocolate pastilles. Gently stir until a smooth consistency is reached and the temperature has reduced to about 40 °C. Then fold in the softly whipped cream.

Mix all the ingredients for the granita together in a shallow freezer-proof container. Place in the freezer but check after an hour or so and loosen with a fork as the ice crystals form.

Divide the crème of white chocolate into four cocktail glasses. Segment the pink grapefruit and arrange on top of the crème. Finish off with the granita and a few sprigs of verbena.

### INGREDIENTS

*Crème of white chocolate*
30 g egg yolks............................
12 g white sugar........................
70 ml semi skimmed milk......
70 ml whipping cream...........
300 g white chocolate
(pastilles) ......................................
3.5 g gelatine leaves ................
500 ml softly whipped,
whipping cream ......................

*Granita*
250 ml Canada Dry.................
50 ml Mombasa Club Gin ......
1 star anise .................................
30 ml ginger syrup..................
50 ml sweet white wine..........
2 pink grapefruits ...................
a few sprigs fresh
lemon verbena.........................

# 12 MUST-VISIT BARS

## BAR SALON
### (ROCK FORT)
BELGIUM - BRUGES

WWW.ROCK-FORT.BE

The trendy restaurant 'Rock Fort' opened its doors in 2001 under the direction of the chefs Peter Laloo and Hermes Vanliefde. As both are mad about Barcelona, they opened a classy tapas bar 'Bar Salon' next door, which has since been incorporated into the restaurant itself. Not the biggest bar, but big on creativity. Bar Salon is not your typical tapas bar, but a fine piece of clever design where gin takes pride of place. A classic gin & tonic or a creative gin cocktail, often with an equally inspiring name; they are clearly mixed with passion. Their gin menu, or 'Gin Mania', features resounding recipes such as 'A'mer, bittere amer met ziltige à la mer': Gin Mare, seaweed and bitter lemon; and 'Gingerito, mojito 3.0': Sipsmith, mint and ginger ale. Hermes accompanies the gin with all sorts of straightforward dishes. One thing is certain; all the creations are just as charismatic as the managers themselves.

# BAR VOLTA GENT

## BELGIUM - GHENT
WWW.VOLTA-GENT.BE

Erik Veldhuis and co-star Ben Wouters have experimentation in their blood. Despite always remaining faithful to their discipline of shaking cocktails, gin & tonic is definitely their permanent mistress. As an ex-pat, Dutchman Erik is happy to make use of his background and history: his favourite gin & tonic is therefore Zuidam Dutch Courage with Fever-Tree Tonic and a long twist of lemon zest and a slice of orange. Bar Volta is above the restaurant of the same name. Housed in a former electrical transformer station, the restaurant is named after Alessandro Volta, the inventor of the battery. The atmosphere crackles and is full of energy, just as power surges through the gin & tonics. The jazzy lounge music completes the picture.

# PURE C

## THE NETHERLANDS - CADZAND
WWW.STRANDHOTEL.EU

It is Sergio Herman (Chef, Oud Sluis***) who has put gin & tonic on the menu in Flanders and The Netherlands. Back in 2005, Sergio or his maître sommelier at the time, used to travel to London twice a week to score some Hendrick's Gin. Whilst bars and nightclubs at that time were only serving the classics, Sergio was also discovering the different varieties of gin in Spain. Barman and mixologist Paul Morel takes his inspiration from Sergio's approach, namely his use of fresh herbs and spices, and applies this to his cocktails. Paul goes beyond the boundaries with his cocktail creations with boundless energy, using products from the local area and techniques from the kitchens of Pure C. Taste the beauty of the sea in Paul's gin & tonic with Oxley Gin, Fever-Tree Indian Tonic Water, sea buckthorn and salty twigs.

# BRISTOL BAR

## SPAIN - MADRID
WWW.BRISTOLBAR.ES

Owners Ellie (United Kingdom) and Fran (Spain) embody Spanish gin culture in their Bristol Bar. The variety of gins on offer is overwhelming and the atmosphere is buzzing. The décor of the interior of the Bristol bar is 'old school', with a black and white marble topped bar, Bordeaux red leather sofas and a life-size portrait of Queen Victoria on the wall. But isn't old school the new cool?! Gin is the order of the day here. All the 'usual suspects' can be found on the menu, but there are also a few gems to discover. Above all, Bristol Bar has its very own gin, and also its own cocktail lounge, 'Gintonize'. Modern Spanish dishes sit comfortably alongside your favourite gin & tonic and if the choice is just too difficult to make, the (Ellie) Baker's Top 10 Gin & Tonic will offer you solace. You should definitely try the 'Royal Pink-Ish' specially designed for the wedding of Prince William and Kate Middleton. This gin & tonic combines Ish Gin, Schweppes Original Premium Tonic Water and cranberry juice, finished off with lime and half a strawberry.

# BOBBY GIN

## SPAIN – BARCELONA
WWW.BOBBYGIN.COM

"The perfect gin & tonic does not exist" is written on one of the walls of Bobby Gin. Nevertheless, the gin & tonic creations in this bar come pretty close. This place-to-be is managed by Alberto Pizaro, award-winning mixologist and bartender par excellence. From the most delicious gin & tonics, to smoked cocktails and various infusions of botanical deliciousness, Bobby Gin is one of the must-visit bars in Barcelona for every gin lover. The retro interior is warm and welcoming. Certainly try out 'Bobby's Spring': a gin & tonic with Bobby's Spring Gin (an in-house creation of a variety of gins with an infusion of hibiscus flower and olive tree leaf), Schweppes Heritage Indian Tonic Water, finished off with strawberry and grapefruit zest.

# 41°

## SPAIN - BARCELONA
WWW.TICKETSBAR.ES

The name El Bulli will possibly ring a few bells: prestigious chef and owner of the legendary restaurant, Ferran Adrià and his brother Albert opened the tapas bar Tickets and the cocktail bar 41° in 2011. You can't miss the place with its bright light boxes and the enormous 'Tickets' sign sparking curiosity as to what's happening inside. However accessible Tickets appears from the outside, it is much more difficult to locate a seat inside as it is always packed. Luckily it is far easier to score a bar stool in the cocktail bar 41°. As the bar is in the same building as Tickets, you can enjoy some must-eat tapas to complement the fantastic gin and tonics.

# GRAPHIC BAR

## UNITED KINGDOM - LONDON

WWW.GRAPHICBAR.COM

This gin bar in Soho offers more than 100 gin varieties. The entire length of the bar is filled almost exclusively with gins, and the menu or rather 'gin bible' provides information on every gin they have available. Graphic Bar houses, in their own words, the biggest gin collection in the world, and strives to serve the perfect Gin & Tonic and Martini: these two cocktails don't mask the taste of the gin. Moreover, you will always find the right tonic and the right garnish with every gin. Art meets bar in Graphic as the décor changes regularly, each time assembled by a different, trendy artist. Graphic Bar is one of the first 'gin-craze' bars in London and they are very happy to work with staff from the Iberian Peninsula, so as to take gin & tonic to a new level.

# PORTOBELLO STAR

## UNITED KINGDOM - LONDON
WWW.PORTOBELLOSTARBAR.CO.UK

The first bar with its own gin, namely Portobello Road N°171, is located in the Notting Hill area. From the outside it looks just like a regular English pub, and it is not immediately apparent that there is a real cocktail bar inside. And to be fair, the inside décor of the Portobello Star is very pub-like. But the cocktails and the gin & tonics are of an extremely high quality. Mixologist Jake Burger definitely knows his trade. Gin lovers can also book a 'Ginstitute' session, which includes a tour of the mini gin museum, followed by a comprehensive history lesson and an introduction to the development of gin. Last but not least, you get the chance to try out your own gin formula.

# THE STAR AT NIGHT

## UNITED KINGDOM - LONDON
WWW.THESTARATNIGHT.COM

The Start at Night in the heart of Soho is the base of the London Gin Club, founded in March 2012. The bar itself was opened in 1933 and has kept much of its original charm. Discover more than seventy gin varieties, including their own 7 Dials London Dry Gin. Constantly in search of premium gins and super-premium gins you can taste the exclusivity. The focus of this bar is, without a doubt, on the quality, and the 'gin menu' is constantly kept up-to-date. Every gin & tonic is served in a 'coppa' glass and matched with the right tonic and garnish. The signature gin is undeniably the 7 Dials Gin with Fever-Tree Indian Tonic Water and frozen raspberries which are 'cracked' by hand.

## GOLDENE BAR

### GERMANY – MUNICH
WWW.GOLDENEBAR.DE

High end and rock & roll go hand in hand at this award-winning (including, amongst others, Bar des Jahres 2013, Mixology Bar Award 2012 and 2013) bar. The bar opened under the management of head barman Klaus Stephan Rainer in 2010, in the 'Haus der Kunst' (House of Art). Classic and modern cocktails complement an innovative food concept under the direction of Chef Michael Heid. A top cocktail bar with an extensive menu, somewhat hidden behind an historic façade, and DJ sets, surfers and celebrities ensure a sizzling atmosphere. Klaus Stephan introduced the idea of adding aromatic homemade tea blends to gin & tonic, creating a type of gin & tonic tea. Many bartenders follow a workshop to develop their own blend. One certainly worth a try is the '24h Ginmillo Tea'. This is an infused gin (Tanqueray N°10) with chamomile, topped up with warm Fever-Tree Indian Tonic Water and finished off with sugar candy.

# GIN & TONIC BAR

GERMANY - BERLIN
WWW.AMANOGROUP.DE/EN/EAT-DRINK/GIN-TONIC-BAR

What's in a name? Yes indeed, this bar in the Amano Hotel in Berlin serves fantastic gin & tonics. According to the Gin & Tonic Bar, the king of cocktails is perfect after work, during dinner, or as a night cap. You can expect more surprising innovations with gin as the protagonist. Gin & tonic infused with tea? Yes, in the Gin & Tonic Bar in Berlin you can try this exceptional mix. Head barman Stjepan Sedlar makes sure you won't forget this surprising combination quickly.

# BUGSY'S BAR

## CZECH REPUBLIC - PRAGUE

WWW.BUGSYSBAR.CZ

Bugsy's Bar welcomed its first guests in the autumn of 1995. There was virtually no cocktail culture in the Czech Republic at the time and Mojito sounded more like a swear word than a delicious drink. After 18 months of hard work and shaking and stirring, Bugsy's Bar had already been included in Newsweek's annual supplement list of 'The World's Best Bars' — the only one located in Central and Eastern Europe. Colleagues in the profession also obviously enjoyed their drinks here: this bar was nominated as the first in the Czech Bar Awards Hall of Fame. No wonder then that this friendly bar is also a pioneer in spreading the gin & tonic gospel throughout the Central European region!

# GINCYCLOPEDIA

This list provides a summary of gins currently available worldwide. However, as new gins are popping up almost every week it is by no means exhaustive, rather more of a snapshot of how it is at the moment. It will hopefully prove to be a useful tool for your initial investigations.

*Note: producers are often (deliberately) vague about production information and so this list also has its limitations. Only gins of 40% ABV make it onto the list, as this is our own idiosyncratic bench mark of quality and passion.*

| NAME | Derivatives | Place of origin | Alc% | Year | Brand owner/ distillery | Number of botanicals | (Known) botanicals |
|---|---|---|---|---|---|---|---|
| 1 & 9 GIN | | France | 40 | | Distillerie Des Terres Rouges | 10 | juniper berry, coriander, orris root, orange, cinnamon |
| 5TH DISTILLED GIN | Fire - Red Fruits | Spain | 42 | | Destilleries del Maresme | 4 | blueberries, raspberries, strawberries, blackberries |
| | Wind - Floral | Spain | 42 | | Destilleries del Maresme | 4 | flowers, spices and botanical elements |
| | Earth - Citrus | Spain | 42 | | Destilleries del Maresme | 4 | grapefruit, orange, mandarin, lemon |
| 6 O'CLOCK GIN | | UK | 43 | | Bramley and Gage | 7 | juniper berry, coriander, angelica, orris root, elderflower, orange peel, savory |
| 7D ESSENTIAL LONDON DRY GIN 0.7L | | Spain | 41 | | Comercial S.A. Tello | 12 | juniper berry, bitter orange, thyme, peppermint, cinnamon, lemon, chamomile, spearmint, sweet orange, lavender, mandarin orange, coriander |
| 12 BRIDGES GIN | | USA | 45 | | Integrity Spirits/ Distillery Row | 12 | |
| 12/11 GIN | | Spain | 42.5 | 2011 | Benevento Global/ Destilerías Liber | 11 | juniper berry, cardamom, rosemary, thyme, lemon and mandarin |
| ADLER BERLIN DRY GIN 0,7L | | Germany | 42 | | Preußische Spirituosen Manufaktur | unknown | juniper berry, lavender, coriander, ginger and lemon peel |
| | Adler's Reserve / KPM Edition | | 47 | | | | |
| ADNAMS DISTILLED GIN | | UK | 40 | 2010 | Adnams Brewery | 6 | juniper berry, orris root, coriander seed, cardamom pod, sweet orange peel and hibiscus flower - See more at: http://adnams.co.uk/spirits/our-spirits/distilled-gin/#sthash.ARyNwTPb.dpuf |
| | Adnams First Rate Gin 0.7L | | 48 | | | | |
| | Adnams Sloe Gin | | 26 | | | | |

| NAME | Derivatives | Place of origin | Alc% | Year | Brand owner/ distillery | Number of botanicals | (Known) botanicals |
|---|---|---|---|---|---|---|---|
| **ALAMBICS GIN (13YO)** | | Scotland, UK | 65.6 | | Alambics Classique | unknown | |
| **ARCTIC VELVET PREMIUM GIN** | | Greenland/ Switzerland | 40 | | ThoCon AG | 25 | juniper berry, coriander, caraway seed, nutmeg |
| **AVIATION GIN** | | USA | 42 | | The House Of Spirits distillery | unknown | lavender, indian sarsaparilla |
| **A.V. VAN WEES THREE CORNER GIN** | | The Netherlands | 42 | | Van Wees | 2 | juniper berry and lemon |
| **BAHIA GIN** | | Spain | 40 | 2011 | Kiskaarly S.L. | 12 | lemom, sweet & bitter orange |
| **BARR HILL GIN** | | USA | 45 | | Caledonia Spirits | unknown | juniper berry, honey |
| **BAYSWATER GIN** | | Spain | 43 | | Casalbor | unknown | juniper berry, coriander seed, angelica root, orris powder, lemon peel, orange peel, lquorice, cassia and nutmeg |
| **BEDROCK GIN** | | UK | 40 | | Spirit Of The Lakes | unknown | juniper berry, coriander seed, lemon and orange peel, angelica root, liquorice root powder and cinnamon |
| **BEEFEATER** | | UK | 40 | | Pernod Ricard/ Beefeater Distillery | 9 | juniper berry, angelica root, angelica seeds, coriander seeds, liquorice, almonds, orris root, seville oranges, and lemon peel |
| | Beefeater24 | | 45 | | | 12 | |
| | Beefeater's Burrough's Reserve | | | | | | |
| | WET by Beefeater | | | | | | |
| | Beefeater London Market (Limited Edition) | | 40 | | | | |
| **BELLRINGER GIN** | | USA | 47 | | Frank-Lin Distillers Products Ltd | unknown | |
| **BIERCÉE GIN** | | Belgium | 44 | | Biercée | 18 | poppies, cocoa, fresh fruit, juniper berry, cloves, hops, hyfope, ambrette, angelica root, cumin, caraway, fennel, coriander, malt wine, vanilla, lavender, amis vert |
| **BIG GIN** | | USA | 47 | | Captive Spirits | 9 | juniper berry, coriander, bitter orange peel, grains of paradise, angelica, cassia, cardamom, orris, Tasmanian pepper berry |
| **BIG BEN DELUXE LONDON DRY GIN** | | India | 42.8 | | Mohan Meakin Ltd / Solan brewery | unknown | |
| **SALICORNIA OCEAN/ TIDES GIN** | | Spain | 40 | | Blanc Gastronomy | 11 | juniper berry, gentian, coriander, angelica root, verbena (lemon verbena), cinnamon, orange, lemon, citrus aurantium (bitter orange), bergamot and samphire |
| **BERKELEY SQUARE GIN** | | UK | 40 | | G&J Greenall | 8 | juniper berry, coriander, basil, angelica root, lavender, cubebs, kaffir lime leaves and sage |
| **BLACK GIN** | | Germany | 45 | | Gansloser Distillerie | 74 | |

| NAME | Derivatives | Place of origin | Alc% | Year | Brand owner/ distillery | Number of botanicals | (Known) botanicals |
|---|---|---|---|---|---|---|---|
| | Black Gin Distiller's Cut | | 60 | | | | |
| | Black Gin Edition 1905 | | 45 | | | | |
| **BLACK DEATH GIN** | | UK | 40 | | G&J Greenall | unknown | |
| **BLACKWOOD'S VINTAGE DRY GIN** | | Shetland Islands, UK | 40 | | Blavod Drinks Ltd | 13 | wild water mint, angelica root, sea pinks, juniper berry, meadow sweet, coriander, cinnamon, liquorice, citrus peel, nutmeg, oris root, violet flowers, turmeric |
| | Blackwood's Vintage Dry Gin | | 60 | | | | |
| **BLADE GIN** | | USA | 47 | | Old World Spirits | 5 | cardamom, juniper berry, lemon peel, orange peel and pepper |
| **BLOOM PREMIUM LONDON DRY GIN** | | UK | 40 | | GJ Greenall's | 4 | juniper berry, honeysuckle, chamomile and pomelo |
| **BLOOMSBURY** | Lemon | UK | 45 | | Bloomsbury Wine & Spirit | unknown | |
| | Orange | UK | 45 | | | | |
| **BLUE GIN** | | Austria | 43 | | Reisetbauer | 27 | lemon rind, angelica root, cilantro seeds, turmeric, liquorice |
| **BLUE RIBBON** | | Spain | 40 | | | 14 | juniper berry, thyme, coriander, orris root, jamaican pepper, citrus, anise, allspice, cinnamon, nutmeg |
| **BLUECOAT GIN** | | USA | 47 | 2007 | Philadelphia Distilling | secret | juniper berry, orange peel, lemon peel, 3rd citrus peel - "more than 6 and less than 20" |
| **BOË SUPERIOR GIN** | | Scotland, UK | 47 | | VC2 brands | 14 | juniper berry, coriander, angelica, ginger, orris root, cassia bark, chinese cinnamon, grains of paradise, orange and lemon peel, cardamom seeds, liquorice, almonds, cubeb berry |
| **BOMBAY SAPPHIRE** | | UK | 40 | 1987 | Bacardi-Martini/ G&J Greenall | 10 | almond, lemon peel, liquorice, juniper berry, orris root, angelica, coriander, cassia, cubeb and grains of paradise |
| | Bombay Dry | | 40 | 2010 | | | |
| | Bombay Sapphire East | | 42 | 2012 | | 12 | |
| **BOODLES GIN** | | UK | 40 | | Proximo Spirits/ G&J Greenall | 9 | juniper berry, coriander seed, angelica root, angelica seed, cassia bark, caraway seed, nutmeg, rosemary, sage |
| **BOTANIC PREMIUM LONDON DRY GIN** | | | 40 | | Williams & Hurbert / Langley Distillery | 14 | buddha's hand, juniper berry, tangerine, thyme, coriander, lemon, cinnamon, peppermint, chamomile, aniseed, sweet orange, almond, cardamom, mango |
| | Botanic Ultra Premium London Dry Gin 0,7L | | 45 | | | | |
| **BOTANICAL AND HOPPY GIN** | | Denmark | 44 | | Mikkeller Spirits/ Braunstein Distillery | unknown | juniper berry, lemon grass, angelica root, cardamom, oranges, hops |
| **BOTH'S OLD TOM GIN** | | Germany | 47 | | Haromex / The Both Distillery | unknown | |

| NAME | Derivatives | Place of origin | Alc% | Year | Brand owner/ distillery | Number of botanicals | (Known) botanicals |
|---|---|---|---|---|---|---|---|
| **BOUDIER GIN** | | France | 40 | | Gabriel Boudier | unknown | |
| | Boudier Sloe Gin | | 25 | | | | |
| **BRECON SPECIAL RESERVE GIN** | | UK | 40 | | Penderyn Distillery | 11 | Welsh Spirit, juniper berry, orange peel, cassia bark, liquorice, cinnamaon bark, angelica root, nutmeg, corianders seeds, lemon peel, orris root |
| **BROCKMANS GIN** | | UK | 40 | | Brockmans Distillery | 10 | juniper berry, coriander, blueberries, blackberries, orange peel |
| **BROKER'S PREMIUM LONDON DRY GIN** | | UK | 40 | 1998 | Broker's Gin Ltd/ Langley Distillery | 10 | juniper berry, coriander, angelica root, orris root, cassia bark, cinnamon, liquorice, nutmeg, orange peel, lemon peel |
| **BULLDOG GIN** | | UK | 40 | 2006 | Bulldog Gin Company/ G&J Greenall | 12 | juniper berry, dragon fruit, poppy, lavender, lotus leaves, coriander, angelica root, orris root, cassia bark, almond, liquorice, lemon peel |
| | Bulldog Gin Extra Bold | | 47 | | | | |
| **BUTLER'S GIN** | | UK | 40 | | Ross William Butler | 10 | juniper berry, fresh lemongrass, cardamom, coriander, cloves, cinnamon, star anise, fennel, lemon and lime |
| **CADENHEAD'S CLASSIC GIN** | | | 50 | | | | |
| **CADENHEAD'S OLD RAJ** | | Scotland, UK | 46 | | WM Cadenhead's | unknown | juniper berry, saffron |
| | Cadenhead's Sloe Gin | | 46 | | | | |
| | Cadenhead's Old Raj | | 55 | | | | |
| **CAORUNN SMALL BATCH GIN** | | Scotland | 41.8 | | Balmenach Distillery | 6 | juniper berry, rowan red berry, heather, bog myrtle, dandelion, apple |
| **CAP ROCK ORGANIC GIN** | | USA | 41 | | Peak Spirits | 12 | juniper berry, apple, lavender, roses |
| **CARDINAL GIN** | | USA | 42 | 2010 | Southern Artisan Spirits | 11 | angelica, apricot kernals, cardamom, cloves, coriander, frankinsence, juniper berry, mint, orange, orris root, spearmint |
| **CASTLE GIN** | The First | Switzerland | 43 | | MQ Wines | unknown | |
| | The Roses | | 43 | | | | |
| **CHASE ELEGANT CRISP GIN** | | | 48 | | Chase Distillery | 10 | juniper berry, coriander, angelica, liquorice, orris, orange, lemon, hops, elderflower and bramley apple |
| | Extra Dry Gin | | 40 | | | 10 | juniper berry, cinnamon, nutmeg, ginger, almond, coriander, cardamom, cloves, liquorice and lemon |
| | Seville Orange Gin | | | | | | |
| | Summer Fruit Cup | | | | | | elderflowers, raspberries and blackcurrants |
| **CHIEF GOWANU NEW-NETHERLAND GIN** | | USA | 44 | 2013 | New York Distilling Company | unknown | juniper berry, cluster hops |

| NAME | Derivatives | Place of origin | Alc% | Year | Brand owner/ distillery | Number of botanicals | (Known) botanicals |
|---|---|---|---|---|---|---|---|
| **CITADELLE GIN** | | France | 44 | 1998 | Cognac Ferrand | 19 | juniper berry, coriander, almond, cassia bark, cardamom, paradise seeds, violets, fennel, cinnamon |
| | Citadelle Réserve Gin (6-9MO) | | 44.7 | 2008 | | | |
| **CITY OF LONDON DRY GIN** | | UK | 40 | 2012 | City of London Distillery | 7 | juniper berry, coriander seed, angelica root, liquorice root and fresh oranges, lemons and pink grapefruit |
| | City of London 'Square Mile Gin' | | 40+ | | | | |
| **COLD RIVER TRADITIONAL GIN** | | USA | 47 | 2010 | Maine Distilleries | 7 | juniper berry, coriander, lemon peel, orange peel, orris root, angelica root and cardamom |
| **COOL GIN** | | Spain | 42.5 | 2011 | Benevento Global/ Destilerías Liber | 12 | |
| **CORSAIR ARTISAN GIN** | | USA | 46 | | Corsair Artisan Distillery | unknown | angelica, coriander, juniper berry, lemon, orange, orris root |
| **CREMORNE 1859 COLONEL FOX DRY GIN** | | UK | 40 | | Cask Liquid Marketing/ Thames Distillery | 6 | juniper berry, coriander, angelica, cassia, liquorice and bitter orange peel |
| **DAMRAK GIN** | | The Netherlands | 41.3 | | Bols | 17 | juniper berry, citrus, honeysuckle |
| **DANCING PINE GIN** | | USA | 40 | | Dancing Pine Distillery | 6 | |
| **DARNLEY'S VIEW GIN** | | Scotland, UK | 40 | 2010 | Wemyss Whisky Company | 6 | juniper berry, lemon peel, coriander seed, angelica root, elderflower and orris root |
| | Darnley's View Spiced Gin | | 42.7 | 2012 | | | |
| **DEATH'S DOOR GIN** | | USA | 47 | | Death's Door Spirits | 3 | juniper berry, coriander and fennel |
| **DESERT JUNIPER GIN** | | USA | 41 | 1998 | Desert Juniper Company/ Bendistillery | unknown | |
| **DH KRAHN GIN** | | USA | 40 | | American Gin Company | 6 | coriander seed, galangal (ginger), grapefruit, juniper berry, lemon peel and orange peel. |
| **COLOMBIAN AGED GIN** | White | Colombia | 43 | 2013 | Destileria Columbiana | unknown | |
| | Dark / Gold | | 43 | 2013 | | | |
| **DINGLE GIN** | | Ireland | 42.5 | 2013 | Dingle Distillery | unknown | juniper berry, rowan berry, angelica, coriander, rowan, fuschia, bog myrtle, heather, chervil and hawthorn |
| **DIPLOME DRY GIN** | | France | 44 | | BeBoDrinks | unknown | juniper berry, coriander, whole lemons, orange peel, angelica, safron,orris root, fennel |
| **DOROTHY PARKER GIN** | | USA | 40 | 2013 | New York Distilling Company | unknown | elderberries, dried hibiscus petals, cinnamon and citrus |
| **EDGERTON ORIGINAL PINK DRY GIN** | | UK | 47 | | Edgerton Distillers Ltd | 14 | pomegranate, coriander, angelica, juniper berry, orris root, sweet orange peel, cassia bark, nutmeg, damiana herb, grains of paradise |

| NAME | Derivatives | Place of origin | Alc% | Year | Brand owner/ distillery | Number of botanicals | (Known) botanicals |
|---|---|---|---|---|---|---|---|
| **EDINBURGH GIN** | | Scotland, UK | 43 | | Spencerfield | 9 | juniper berry, coriander, angelica root, orris root, lemon peel, pine cone, heather, thistle |
| | Raspberry Gin | | | | | | |
| | Elderflower | | | | | | |
| **ENTROPIA GIN** | | Spain | 40 | | Entropia Liquors | unknown | juniper berry, coriander, ginseng, guarana, hibiscus, orange peel, lemon peel, liquorice root, nutmeg |
| **ETHEREAL GIN** | | USA | 43 | | Berkshire Mountain Distillers | unknown | changes every batch |
| **FARMER'S ORGANIC GIN** | | USA | 46.7 | | Crop Harvest Earth Co | secret | juniper berry, elderflower, lemon grass, coriander, angelica root |
| **FAHRENHEIT GIN** | | France | 40 | | Gabriel Boudier | unknown | juniper berry, coriander, orange & lemon peel, angelica seed, orris, fennel |
| **FEW AMERICAN GIN** | | USA | 40 | 2011 | FEW Spirits | 11 | juniper berry, citrus (lemon & orange peel), Tahitian vanilla, cassia, grains-of-paradise and homegrown hops |
| | Barrel Aged Gin (4MO) | | 46.5 | | | | |
| **FIFTY POUNDS GIN** | | UK | 43.5 | | Fifty Pounds Co | unknown | juniper berry, coriander, savory, grains of paradise, orange & lemon peel, liquorice, angelica root |
| **FILLIERS DRY GIN 28** | | Belgium | 46 | | Filliers Graanstokerij | 28 | |
| | Filliers Dry Gin 28 Tangerine Seasonal Edition | | 43.7 | | | | |
| **FG 20-3** | | Belgium | 46 | 2012 | Stokerij De Moor | 23 | |
| **FOXDENTON DRY GIN** | | UK | 48 | 2009 | Foxdenton Estate Company | unknown | juniper berry, angelica root, orris root, coriander seeds, lemon peel, lime flower |
| | Foxdenton Blackjack Gin | | | | | | |
| | Foxdenton Raspberry Gin | | | | | | |
| | Foxdenton Damson Gin | | | | | | |
| | Foxdenton Sloe Gin | | | | | | |
| **G&CIN** | | Spain | 40 | | Destilerías Acha | unknown | |
| **G/10** | | France | 40 | | Hervé Erard Spirits | 10 | |
| **GALE FORCE GIN** | | USA | 44.4 | | Triple Eight Distillery | unknown | anise, cassia, juniper berry, lemon, lemongrass, mint, orange |
| **GERANIUM GIN** | | UK | 44 | | Hammer & Son | unknown | juniper berry, geranium oil, coriander, lemon peel, angelica root, orris root, anise, cinnamon |
| **GET BACK GIN** | Blue Gin | Spain | 40 | | Destilerías Acha | unknown | |
| | Pink Gin | | 40 | | | | |
| **GILPIN'S EXTRA DRY GIN** | | UK | 47 | | Westmorland Spirits Ltd | 6 | juniper berry, sage, borage, 3 citrus peels |

| NAME | Derivatives | Place of origin | Alc% | Year | Brand owner/ distillery | Number of botanicals | (Known) botanicals |
|---|---|---|---|---|---|---|---|
| **GIN MARE** | | Spain | 42.7 | | Global Premium Brands | 5 | juniper berry, thyme, basil, rosemary, olives |
| **GIN SEA** | | Spain | 40 | | Manuel Barrientos | 10 | juniper berry, cardamom, coriander, thyme, chamomile, liquorice, peppermint, lemon, sweet orange, bitter orange |
| **GINSELF** | | Spain | 40 | | Gin Al Punto | 9 | sweet orange, bitter orange, lemon peel, angelica root, angelica seed, orange blossom, tiger nut, juniper berry & mandarin |
| **GLORIOUS GIN** | | USA | 45 | 2010 | Breuckelen Distilling | 5 | juniper berry, lemon, rosemary, ginger, grapefruit |
| **GOLDEN MOON GIN** | | USA | 45 | | Golden Moon Distillery | unknown | |
| **GREENALL'S LONDON DRY GIN** | | UK | 40 | 1760 | G&J Greenall Distillers | 8 | juniper berry, coriander, lemon peel, angelica, orris, liquorice, cassia bark and bitter almonds |
| **GREENBRIER GIN** | | USA | 40 | | Smooth Ambler Spirits | unknown | citrus peel, juniper berry and pepper |
| **GREEN HAT GIN** | | USA | 41.1 | | New Columbia Distillers | unknown | juniper berry, citrus, coriander, grains of paradise, celery seed |
| **GREYLOCK GIN** | | USA | 40 | | Berkshire Mountain Distillers | 7 | |
| **GUGLHOF ALPIN GIN** | | Austria | 42 | 2010 | Brennerei Guglhof | unknown | blackberries, flour berries, alpine rose bleed |
| **GILT GIN** | | Scotland, UK | 40 | | Gilt Gin Co | unknown | |
| **GOLD 999.9** | | Spain | 40 | | The Water Company | 10 | tangerine, almonds, ginger, violet, coriander, angelica root, cinnamon, gentian, poppy, juniper berry |
| **G-VINE** | Floraison | France | 40 | | EuroWineGate | 10 | vine flower, juniper berry, ginger, liquorice, cassia bark, green cardamom, coriander, cubeb berries, nutmeg and lime |
| | Nouaison | | 43.9 | | | 10 | vine blossom, juniper berry, ginger, liquorice, cassia bark, green cardamom, coriander, cubeb berries, nutmeg and lime |
| **HANA GIN** | | USA | 40 | | Branded Spirits | unknown | |
| **HASWELL LONDON DRY GIN** | | UK | 47 | | Rainbow Chaser Ltd | 9 | juniper berry, angelica, coriander, savory, lemon peel, grains of pardise, bitter orange peel, sweet orange peel, liquorice |
| **HAYMAN'S LONDON DRY GIN** | | UK | 40 | | Hayman Distillers | 10 | unknown |
| | Hayman's 1820 Gin Liqueur | | 40 | | | | |
| | Hayman's 1850 Reserve Gin (5WO) | | 40 | | | | |
| | Hayman's Old Tom Gin | | 40 | | | | |

| NAME | Derivatives | Place of origin | Alc% | Year | Brand owner/ distillery | Number of botanicals | (Known) botanicals |
|---|---|---|---|---|---|---|---|
| | Hayman's City of London | | 40 | | | | |
| | Hayman's Royal Dock Gin | | 57 | | | | |
| | Hayman's Sloe Gin | | 26 | | | | |
| **HENDRICK'S GIN** | | Scotland, UK | 41.5 | | William Grant & Sons Ltd | 11 | extra infusion of rose petals & cucumber |
| **HERNÖ GIN** | | Sweden | 40.5 | 2012 | Hernö Brenneri | 8 | juniper berry, coriander, meadowsweet, cassia, black pepper, vanilla, lemon peel, lingonberries |
| | Hernö Navy Strength | | 57 | 2013 | | | |
| | Hernö Juniper Cask Gin | | | 2013 | | | |
| **HOXTON GIN** | | UK | 43 | | Gerry Calabrese | unknown | coconut, grapefruit, juniper berry, orris, tarragon and Ginger |
| **SPIRIT OF HVEN ORGANIC GIN** | | Sweden | 40 | | Spirit of Hven Distillery | unknown | juniper berry, grains of paradise, citrus, Sichuan pepper, aniseed, guinea pepper |
| **IMAGIN** | | Sweden | 40 | 2011 | Facile & Co | 12 | |
| **ISFJORD ARCTIC GIN** | | Greenland | 44 | 2007 | Isjford Distillery | 12 | juniper berry, angelica, lemon grass, cardamom, orange |
| **ISH LONDON DRY GIN** | | Spain | 41 | | The Poshmakers | 11 | juniper berry, coriander seed, angelica root, almond, orris root, nutmeg, cinnamon, cassia, liquorice, lemon and orange peel |
| | Ish Limed London Dry Gin | | 41 | | | | |
| **JENSEN'S BERMONDSEY GIN** | | UK | 43 | | Bermondsey Gin Ltd | unknown | coriander, orris root, angelica, liquorice, juniper berry |
| | Jensen's Old Tom Gin | | 43 | | | | |
| **JODHPUR** | | UK | 43 | | Beveland Distillers | 13 | angelica, bitter almonds, coriander, cassia bark, juniper berry, lemon peel, liquorice root, orris root, orange peel, ginger, pomelo peel |
| | Jodhpur Reserve (2YO) | | 43 | | | | |
| **JOSEPHINE GIN** | | France | 40 | | Camus Cognac | unknown | |
| **JUDGES LONDON DRY GIN** | | UK | 40 | | Cale distillers | unknown | |
| **JUNIPER GREEN ORGANIC** | | UK | 43 | | Organics Spirits Co/ Thames Distillers | 4 | juniper berry, coriander, savory and angelica root |
| **JUNIPERO GIN** | | USA | 49.3 | 1996 | Anchor Distilling Company | secret | |
| **K-25** | | Spain | 45 | | Destilerías Acha | unknown | |
| **KNOCKEEN HEATHER GIN** | | UK | 47.3 | | Knockeen Hills | unknown | heather, juniper berry, coriander, angelica root, savoury |
| | Knockeen Hills Elderflower Gin | | 43 | | | | |

| NAME | Derivatives | Place of origin | Alc% | Year | Brand owner/ distillery | Number of botanicals | (Known) botanicals |
|---|---|---|---|---|---|---|---|
| **LARIOS (12) PREMIUM GIN** | | Spain | 40 | | Beam Global | 12 | juniper berry, nutmeg, angelica root, coriander, Mediterranean lemon, orange, tangerine, mandarin, clementine, grapefruit, lime and orange blossom |
| **LEBENSSTERN DRY GIN** | | Germany | 43 | | Lebensstern Bar/ Freihof Distillery | unknown | |
| | Lebensstern Pink Gin | | 43 | | | | |
| **LEOPOLD'S AMERICAN SMALL BATCH GIN** | | USA | 40 | 2002 | Leopold Brothers | 5 | juniper berry, coriander, orris root, California pomelos, Valencia oranges |
| **LEVEL PREMIUM GIN** | | Spain | 44 | | Teichenné | 8 | |
| **LIGHTHOUSE BATCH DISTILLED GIN** | | New Zealand | 42 | | Greytown Fine Distillates | 9 | secret |
| | Hawthorn Edition | | 57 | | | | |
| **LONDON HILL DRY GIN** | | UK | 43 | 1785 | Ian Macleod Distillers/ Langley Distillery | unknown | juniper berry, citrus peels and coriander seeds |
| **LONDON N° 1 ORIGINAL BLUE GIN** | | Spain | 47 | | Gonzalez Byass | 13 | juniper berry, anglica, cinnamon, almonds, coriander |
| **LUBUSKI GIN** | Classic Gin | Poland | 40 | 1987 | Henkell & Co. Vinpol/ Lubuski Distillery | 14 | juniper berry, coriander, angelica root, citrus peel, liquorice, cassia bark, bitter almonds, cardamom, cinnamon, star anise, cumin, calamus (myrtle), marigold flowers, bay leaf |
| | Lime Gin | | 40 | | | | |
| **M5 GIN** | | Spain | 48 | | Bodegas Vinícola Real | 26 | |
| **MG 1835 ORIGINAL DRY GIN** | | Spain | 43 | | Destilerías MG | unknown | |
| **MACARONESIAN (WHITE) GIN** | | Spain | 40 | | Destileria Santa Cruz | unknown | juniper berry, cardamom, angelica root, liquorice, lemon peel, orange peel |
| **MAGELLAN BLUE GIN** | | France | 44 | | Angeac Distillery | 11 | cloves, cinnamon, coriander, cardamom, orris root & flower, cassia, liquorice, juniper berry, orange peel, grains of paradise, nutmeg |
| **MARTIN MILLER'S DRY GIN** | | UK | 40 | 1999 | The Reformed Spirits Co | 10 | Florentine iris, juniper berry, cassia bark, liquorice, coriander, angelica root, bitter orange peel, lemon peel, lime peel, cucumber |
| | Martin Millers, 'Westbourne Strength,' Dry Gin | | 45.2 | 2003 | | | |
| **MASCARO GIN 9** | | Spain | 40 | 2010 | Antonio Mascaro | 1 | juniper berry |
| **MASONS YORKSHIRE DRY GIN** | | UK | 42 | | Karl Mason | unknown | |
| **MASTER'S SELECTION** | | Spain | 40 | | Destilerías MG | unknown | |
| **MAYFAIR LONDON DRY GIN** | | UK | 40 | | Mayfair Brands/ Thames Distillery | 5 | juniper berry, coriander, angelica, orris, savoury |

| NAME | Derivatives | Place of origin | Alc% | Year | Brand owner/ distillery | Number of botanicals | (Known) botanicals |
|---|---|---|---|---|---|---|---|
| **MOMBASA CLUB LONDON DRY GIN** | | UK | 41.5 | | Imperial British East Africa Company | unknown | juniper berry, angelica root, coriander seeds, cassia bark |
| **MONKEY 47 DRY GIN** | | Germany | 47 | | Black Forest Distillers | 47 | |
| | Monkey 47 Sloe Gin | | 47 | | | | |
| | Monkey 47 Distillers Cut | | 47 | | | | |
| **MONOPOLOWA VIENNA DRY GIN** | | Austria | 44 | | Altvater Gessler - J.A. Baczewski | unknown | caraway seed, coriander seed, fennel seed, ginger, lemon peel and orange peel. |
| **MYER FARM GIN** | | USA | 42.7 | | Myer Farm Distillers | 10 | juniper berry, coriander, cinnamon and citrus |
| **MYRTLE GIN (10YO)** | | Scotland, UK | 47 | | Spirit of the Coquet | unknown | Northumberland myrtle |
| **NEW AMSTERDAM GIN** | | USA | 40 | | New Amsterdam Spirits Co | 20 | |
| **N°0 LONDON DRY** | | Spain | 41 | | Number Zero Drinks | 11 | juniper berry, coriander, angelica, lavender, orris, cinnamon, cinchona (containing the quinine) from Peru |
| **N°209 GIN** | | USA | 46 | | Distillery N°209 | between 8 & 11 | juniper berry, bergamot, orange, lemon peel, cardamom pods, cassia bark, angelica root, coriander seeds |
| **N°3 LONDON DRY GIN** | | The Netherlands | 46 | | De Kuyper Royal Distillers | unknown | |
| **NOLET'S DRY GIN SILVER** | | The Netherlands | 47.6 | | Nolet Distillery | unknown | Turkish rose, peach, raspberry |
| | Nolet's Dry Gin - The Reserve | The Netherlands | 52.3 | | | | |
| **NORDÉS GIN** | | Spain | 40 | | Atlantic Galician Spirits | unknown | verbena, lemon peel, eucalyptus leaves, sage, juniper berry, cardamom, quinine, ginger, hibiscus, liquorice, tea |
| **NORTH SHORE DISTILLER'S GIN** | N°6 & N°11 | USA | 45 | 2007 | North Shore Distillery | unknown | |
| **NUT GIN** | | Spain | | | Emporda | 13 | juniper berry, coriander, cardamom, angelica root, lemon peel, orange peel, green walnuts, fragrant nutmeg, rosemary, thyme, olive tree leaves, cinnamon and liquorice |
| **NUTMEG GIN** | | Austria | 44 | | Oliver Matter/ Erlebnis Brennerei | unknown | |
| **O WANNBORGA GIN** | | Sweden | 40.1 | | Destileria Wannborga | 9 | juniper berry, angelica root, coriander, cardamom, nutmeg, cinnamon, white pepper, lemon peel, bitter orange peel |
| **OLD BUCK GIN** | | South Africa | 43 | | Henry Tayler & Ries Ltd. | unknown | |
| **OLD ENGLISH GIN** | | UK | 44 | | Hammer & Son | unknown | |

| NAME | Derivatives | Place of origin | Alc% | Year | Brand owner/ distillery | Number of botanicals | (Known) botanicals |
|---|---|---|---|---|---|---|---|
| OLD LADY'S GIN | | France | 40 | | Marie Brizard | unknown | |
| OLIVER CROMWELL 1599 PREMIUM GIN | | The Netherlands | 40 | | Aldi Stores Ltd. | unknown | |
| ONE KEY GIN | | Singapore | 40 | | Abnormal Group Singapore | unknown | juniper berry, ginger, coriander, exotic plant extracts |
| ONLY GIN | | Spain | 43 | | Campeny Destilleries | 11 | juniper berry, jasmine, veronica, violet, rose petals, lavender, orange blossom, mallow, pansies, lemon balm, hibiscus |
| ORIGIN SINGLE ESTATE LONDON DRY GIN | UK | UK | 40 | | Master of Malt | 1 | juniper berry |
| | Croatia | | | | | | |
| | Macedonia | | | | | | |
| | Albania | | | | | | |
| | Kosovo | | | | | | |
| | Bulgaria | | | | | | |
| | Italy | | | | | | |
| OXLEY DRY GIN | | UK | 47 | | Oxley Spirits Co | unknown | |
| PALLADIAN DRY GIN | | UK | 40 | | Mayfair Distillery | unknown | |
| PALMERS LONDON DRY GIN | | UK | 40 | | Alcohols Ltd/ Langley Distillery | 10 | unknown |
| PERRY'S TOT NAVY GIN | | USA | 57 | | New York Distilling Company | 8 | juniper berry, cinnamon, cardamom, star anise, lemon, orange & grapefruit peel, wild flower honey |
| PINCKNEY BEND GIN | | USA | 46.5 | | Pinckney Bend Distillery | 9 | juniper berry, coriander seeds, orris root, angelica, liquorice, and three different kinds of dried citrus |
| PINK 47 GIN | | UK | 47 | | Old St Andrews Ltd | 10 | juniper berry, coriander, angelica root (2), lemon peel, orange peel, orris root, liquorice, almond, cassia bark, nutmeg |
| PLYMOUTH GIN | | UK | 41.2 | | Plymouth Distillery | unknown | |
| | Plymouth Gin Navy Strength | UK | 57 | | | | |
| | Plymouth Sloe Gin | UK | | | | | |
| POPPIES GIN | | Belgium | 40 | | Stokerij Rubbens | unknown | poppies |
| PORTOBELLO ROAD N° 171 LONDON DRY GIN | | UK | 42 | | Jake Burger/ Thames Distillers Ltd | unknown | |
| PORT OF DRAGONS | | Spain | 44 | | Premium Distillery | unknown | almond, angelica, anise, cardamom, coriander, ginger, hazelnut, hibiscus, juniper, lemon, lime, liquorice, nutmeg, orange, poppy, rose, vanilla, fennel |

| NAME | Derivatives | Place of origin | Alc% | Year | Brand owner/ distillery | Number of botanicals | (Known) botanicals |
|------|-------------|-----------------|------|------|-------------------------|----------------------|--------------------|
| **PROFESSOR CORNELIUS AMPLEFORTH'S BATHTUB GIN** | | UK | 43.3 | | Master of Malt | unknown | juniper berry, orange peel, coriander, cinnamon, cloves and cardamom |
| **RAFFLES LONDON DRY GIN** | | Scotland, UK | 40 | | William Maxwell Distillery | 13 | juniper berry, coriander seeds, angelica root, orange & lemon peel, cassia bark, ginger, nutmeg, liquorice root, almonds, cinnamon bark, fennel and cardamom seeds |
| **RANSOM OLD TOM GIN (6-9MO)** | | USA | 44 | | Ransom Spirits | 6 | juniper berry, orange peel, lemon peel, coriander seed, cardamom pods and angelica root |
| **REVAL DRY GIN** | | Spain | 40 | | Remedia Distillery | unknown | |
| **RIGHT GIN 0.7L** | | Sweden | 40 | | Altamar Brands/ Right Distillery | unknown | bergamot |
| **ROARING FORTIES GIN** | | New Zealand | 40 | | South Pacific Distillery | unknown | |
| **ROB'S MTN GIN** | | USA | 44 | | Spring44 Distilling Inc | unknown | juniper berry, coriander, orris root, orange peel, kaffir lime leaf, basil, peppermint, Unicorn Tears |
| **ROUNDHOUSE GIN** | | USA | 47 | | Roundhouse Spirits | unknown | juniper berry, coriander, citrus peel, star anise, angelica, orris root, sencha green tea, lavender, hibiscus and chamomile |
| **SACRED GIN** | | UK | 40 | | Sacred Spirits Company | 12 | juniper berry, citrus, cardamom, nutmeg, frankincense |
| | Sacred Cardamom Gin | | | | | | |
| **SAFFRON GIN** | | France | 40 | | Gabriel Boudier | unknown | juniper berry, saffron, coriander, lemon, orange peel, angelica seeds, orris, fennel |
| **SEAGRAM'S EXTRA DRY GIN** | | USA | 40 | | Seagram & Sons | unknown | |
| | Distiller's Reserve (6MO) | | 51 | 2006 | | | |
| **SECRET TREASURES GIN 'OLD TOM STYLE'** | | Germany | 40 | | Haromex | unknown | |
| **SIKKIM INDIAN BRITISH TEA** | Private | Spain | 40 | | | unknown | juniper berry, red tea, floral aromas, coriander |
| | Bilberry | | 40 | | | | juniper berry, red tea, flower essences, blackberries, blueberries, coriander, orris, calamus, bitter orange peel |
| **SIPSMITH LONDON DRY GIN** | | UK | 41.6 | 2009 | Sipsmith Distillery | 10 | Macedonian juniper, Bulgarian coriander seeds, French angelica root, Spanish liquorice root, Italian orris root, Spanish ground almond, Chinese cassia bark, Madagascan cinnamon, Seville orange, Spanish lemon peel |
| | Sipsmith Sloe Gin | | 29 | | | | |
| | Sipsmith Summer Cup | | 29 | | | | |
| | Sipsmith VJOP (Very Juniper Over Proof) | | 52 | | | | |

| NAME | Derivatives | Place of origin | Alc% | Year | Brand owner/ distillery | Number of botanicals | (Known) botanicals |
|---|---|---|---|---|---|---|---|
| | Sipsmith Blue Label | | 44.1 | | | | |
| SLOANE'S DRY GIN | | The Netherlands | 40 | | Toorank Distilleries | 9 | orange, angelica root, orris root, coriander seeds, juniper berry, vanilla, cardamom, liquorice, lemon |
| SOUTH GIN | | New Zealand | 48.2 | 2005 | 42Below | 9 | juniper berry, lemon, orange, coriander seed, angelica leaves, orris root, gentian root, manuka berries, and kawakawa leaves |
| SPIRIT HOUND GIN | | USA | 42 | | Spirit Hound Distillers | 9 | juniper berry, fennel seeds, Sichuan peppercorns, cloves, cinnamon, star anise |
| SPRING GIN | | Belgium | 40 | | Manuel Wouters/ Filliers Graanstokerij | 13 | coriander, lemon and orange peel, star anise, black pepper, cardamom, ginger, rhubarb, pine buds, delicate orange blossom, cinnamon, angelica |
| | Spring Gin Gentleman's Cut | | 48.8 | | | | |
| | Spring Gin Ladies' Edition | | 38.3 | | | | |
| STEED GIN | | UK | 44 | | Cial. Fuente Anguila Ltd | unknown | juniper berry, coriander, angelica root, lemon peel, orange peel, cinnamon, cardamom, Florence lily |
| ST GEORGES GIN | Terroir Gin | USA | 45 | | St George Spirits | unknown | Douglas fir, California bay laurel, coastal sage |
| | Botanivore Gin | | 45 | | | 19 | angelica root, bay laurel, bergamot peel, black peppercorn, caraway, cardamom, cilantro, cinnamon, citra hops, coriander, dill seed, fennel seed, ginger, juniper berry, lemon peel, lime peel, orris root, Seville orange peel, star anise |
| | Dry Rye Gin | | 45 | | | unknown | rye |
| SUAU GIN | | Spain | 43 | | Bodega Suau/ Bodegas y Destillerias de Mallorca | | oranges, lemons, almonds, juniper berry, coriander, angelica, orris, liquorice root |
| SW4 GIN | | UK | 40 | 2009 | Park Place Drinks Ltd/ Thames Distillery | 12 | juniper berry, lemon, orange, coriander, savory, orris powder, cinnamon, cassia, nutmeg, almonds, liquorice root and angelica |
| TANN'S GIN | | Spain | 40 | 1977 | Campeny Destilleries | 10 | juniper berry, coriander, cucumber, rose petals, cardamom, mandarin peel, orange blossom, lemon peel, liquorice, raspberry |
| TANQUERAY DRY GIN | | UK | 40 | | Diageo | 4 | secret |
| | Tanqueray N° Ten Dry Gin | | 47.3 | 2000 | | | |
| | Tanqueray Dry Gin Rangpur | | 41.3 | 2006 | | | |
| | Tanqueray Malacca | | | 1997 | | | |
| TASMANIAN GODFATHER GIN | | Australia | 40 | | Lark Distillery | unknown | pepper berry |

| NAME | Derivatives | Place of origin | Alc% | Year | Brand owner/ distillery | Number of botanicals | (Known) botanicals |
|---|---|---|---|---|---|---|---|
| **THE BITTER TRUTH PINK GIN** | | Germany | 40 | | The Bitter Truth | unknown | |
| | The Bitter Truth Sloeberry Blue Gin | | 28 | | | | |
| **THE BOTANICAL'S LONDON DRY GIN** | | UK | 42.5 | | Langley Distillery | 14 | juniper berry, coriander, cassia, orange, lemon, cinnamon, orris, angelica, liquorice, nutmeg, grapefruit, lemon blossom, orange blossom |
| **THE BOTANIST DRY GIN** | | Scotland, UK | 46 | | Bruichladdich | 22 | orris root, cassia bark, coriander seed |
| **THE DUKE MUNICH DRY GIN** | | Germany | 45 | | The Duke Destillerie | 13 | juniper berry, coriander, lemon peel, angelica root, lavender, ginger, orange blossom, pepper |
| **THE STING GIN** | | UK | 40 | | | 10 | |
| **THE TRADEWINDS 'CUTLASS' GIN** | | Australia | 50 | | Tailor Made Spirits Company | unknown | lemon myrtle |
| **TWO BIRDS COUNTRYSIDE LONDON DRY GIN** | | UK | 40 | 2012 | Union Distillers Ltd | unknown | |
| **UNCLE VAL'S BOTANICAL GIN** | | USA | 43 | | 35 Maple Street | 5 | juniper berry, cucumber, lavender, lemon, sage |
| **UNGAVA PREMIUM CANADIAN GIN** | | Canada | 43.1 | | Ungava Gin Co | 6 | crowberry, wild rose hips, Labrador tea, Arctic blend, cloudberry |
| **VAN GOGH GIN** | | The Netherlands | 47 | 1999 | Royal Dirkzwager Distilleries | 10 | coriander, liquorice, angelica, juniper berry, grains of paradise, almonds, lemons, cassia bark, orris, cubeb berries |
| **VALLENDAR PURE GIN** | | Germany | 40 | | Brennerei Hubertus Vallendar | unknown | |
| **VL-92 GIN** | | The Netherlands | 41.7 | 2011 | Van Toor Distileerderij | unknown | fresh coriander leaves |
| **VONES GIN** | | Spain | 40 | | LAJ Spirits | 11 | juniper berry, coriander, angelica, lemon peel, orange peel, liquorice root, cassia, cinnamon, nutmeg, Florencia root, chestnuts |
| **VOYAGER SMALL-BATCH DRY GIN** | | USA | 42 | | Pacific Distillery | unknown | juniper berry, orris root, citrus, angelica, cardamom and cassia |
| **WHITLEY NEILL DRY GIN** | | UK | 42 | 2005 | Whitley Neill Ltd/ The Sovereign Distillery | 7 | baobab fruit and cape gooseberries |
| **ZEPHYR GIN** | Blu Gin | UK | 40 | | Zephyr Imports | unknown | elderberries, gardenia |
| | Black Gin | | 44 | | | unknown | exotic botanicals |
| **ZUIDAM DRY GIN** | | The Netherlands | 43.5 | | Zuidam Distillers | 9 | angelica root, cardamom, coriander seed, orris root, juniper berry, lemon peel & orange peel |
| | Zuidam Dutch Courage | | 44.5 | | | | |

| NAME | Derivatives | Place of origin | Alc% | Year | Brand owner/ distillery | Number of botanicals | (Known) botanicals |
|---|---|---|---|---|---|---|---|
| | | | | | | | |
| | | | | | | | |
| | | | | | | | |
| | | | | | | | |
| | | | | | | | |
| | | | | | | | |
| | | | | | | | |
| | | | | | | | |
| | | | | | | | |

| NAME | Derivatives | Place of origin | Alc% | Year | Brand owner/distillery | Number of botanicals | (Known) botanicals |
|---|---|---|---|---|---|---|---|
| | | | | | | | |
| | | | | | | | |
| | | | | | | | |
| | | | | | | | |
| | | | | | | | |
| | | | | | | | |
| | | | | | | | |
| | | | | | | | |
| | | | | | | | |

| NAME | Derivatives | Place of origin | Alc% | Year | Brand owner/ distillery | Number of botanicals | (Known) botanicals |
|------|-------------|-----------------|------|------|-------------------------|----------------------|--------------------|
| | | | | | | | |
| | | | | | | | |
| | | | | | | | |
| | | | | | | | |
| | | | | | | | |
| | | | | | | | |
| | | | | | | | |
| | | | | | | | |
| | | | | | | | |

| NAME | Derivatives | Place of origin | Alc% | Year | Brand owner/distillery | Number of botanicals | (Known) botanicals |
|------|-------------|-----------------|------|------|------------------------|----------------------|--------------------|
| | | | | | | | |
| | | | | | | | |
| | | | | | | | |
| | | | | | | | |
| | | | | | | | |
| | | | | | | | |
| | | | | | | | |
| | | | | | | | |
| | | | | | | | |
| | | | | | | | |

## COLOPHON

WWW.LANNOO.COM

*Register on our web site and we will regularly send you
a newsletter with information about new books and
interesting, exclusive offers.*

**Text:**
Frédéric Du Bois, Isabel Boons

**Photography:**
Kris Vlegels,
except for the bottles on pages 45, 56 and 62,
they were delivered by Magnifique brands

**Illustrations:**
Emma Thyssen

**English translation:**
Fran Oosterbaan-Clarke

**Design:**
KIET

If you have questions about gin & tonic
send an e-mail to: info@miraflor.be
If you have observations, please contact our
editorial office: redactielifestyle@lannoo.com

© Uitgeverij Lannoo nv, Tielt, 2014
*Second printrun*

D/2013/45/511 – NUR 447
ISBN: 978 94 014 1423 4

All rights reserved. Nothing from this publication may be copied,
stored in an automated database and/or be made public in any form
or in any way, either electronic, mechanical or in any other manner
without the prior written consent of the publisher.